The Hand of God

The Hand of God

A journey from
death to life by the abortion doctor
who changed his mind

BERNARD NATHANSON, M.D.

REGNERY PUBLISHING, INC.
Washington, D.C.

First paperback edition 2001

Library of Congress Cataloging-in-Publication Data

Nathanson, Bernard N., 1926-
    The hand of God : a journey from death to life by the abortion
doctor who changed his mind / Bernard N. Nathanson.
       p.   cm.
     ISBN 0-89526-174-X
     1. Abortion—Moral and ethical aspects. 2. Abortion—Religious
aspects. I. Title.
    HQ767.15.N379 1996
    363.4'6—dc20   95-26848
                                             CIP

Published in the United States by
Regnery Publishing, Inc.
An Eagle Publishing Company
One Massachusetts Avenue, NW
Washington, DC 20001

Distributed to the trade by
National Book Network
4720-A Boston Way
Lanham, MD 20706

www.regnery.com

Printed on acid-free paper
Manufactured in the United States of America

10 9 8 7 6 5 4 3 2 1

Books are available in quantity for promotional or premium use. Write to Director of Special Sales, Regnery Publishing, Inc., One Massachusetts Avenue, NW, Washington, DC 20001, for information on discounts and terms or call (202) 216-0600.

For all those who have prayed for me—especially Fr. Paul Marx (that saintly man) and Fr. Richard Neuhaus (his mind is a national treasure).

Contents

Acknowledgments

I AM FOREVER AND UNREQUITABLY indebted to Fr. Paul Marx for far too many things to list here—but it was at his kind invitation (and an invitation from this saintly man is a command to me) that I gave the extemporaneous lecture from which this book derives.

Richard Vigilante heard the tape of that lecture and proposed the book. He has been always a source of encouragement and inspiration—especially during the taping sessions we held—and there simply would have been no book without him.

I am deeply indebted to Dr. Richard Zaner, my mentor at the Center for Research and Clinical Ethics at Vanderbilt University. This kindly, brilliant man taught me that it is the questions that are important, not the answers—there is no one (with the possible exception of that infuriating, exasperating troublemaker Socrates) who could ever ask questions like Dr. Zaner. He has been unfailingly patient and understanding with me in a troubling era of my life, and I shall always be in his debt.

Bernard N. Nathanson, M.D.

The Hand of God

CHAPTER I

The Monster

I DID MY LAST ABORTION in late 1978 or early 1979. I was doing only a few abortions in those years, and those only for what I deemed compelling medical reasons. The years that have passed since I routinely performed abortions have been for me a remarkable odyssey—medically, ethically, and finally spiritually. I will probably fumble through some of the words when we get to the spiritual end of my journey.

This book will be semi-autobiographical, using myself as a paradigm for the study of the systematic fission and demise of one system of morality, no matter how fragmented, fatuous, and odious, and the painful acquisition of another more coherent, more reliable, and less atomistic one.

The backdrop will be the issue of abortion. I know the Holocaust well, having studied it intensively and having lost relatives to it. I also have conventional knowledge of marxism and its bloody legacy. But I know the abortion issue as perhaps no one else does.

I know every facet of abortion. I was one of its accoucheurs; I helped nurture the creature in its infancy by feeding it great draughts of blood and money; I guided it through its adolescence as it grew fecklessly out of control. It is said that if we grew at the same rate during our entire gestation as we do in the first two weeks of life we would each weigh twenty-eight thousand pounds at birth. Abortion is now a monster so unimaginably gargantuan that even to think of stuffing it back into its cage (having fattened on the bodies of thirty million humans) is ludicrous beyond words. Yet that is our charge—a herculean endeavor.

At the conclusion of many of my lectures, I am often taken aside and asked: Isn't abortion at the root of all our problems? Hasn't the abortion mentality infiltrated our culture so extensively that it has contaminated every social institution touching upon our lives: education, family, sex, politics, economics? And if abortion were to be recriminalized, would not our moribund society come bounding off its ventilator in robust good health?

The answers are no, yes, and no. The abortion *mentality,* for lack of a better word, has steadily metastasized throughout our society so subtly and so aggressively that even if it were miraculously recriminalized it is extremely doubtful if such allied plagues as child abuse, pornography, violence against women, and genocide (I have my annual physical check-up scheduled with Dr. Kevorkian next week) would all magically vanish.

We live in an age of fulsome nihilism; an age of death; an age in which, as author Walker Percy (a fellow physician, a pathologist who specialized in autopsying Western civilization) argued, "compassion leads to the gas chamber," or the abortion clinic, or the euthanist's office. We live in an age of defining personhood upward so that fewer and fewer of us make the cut, an age of virtual abjuring of moral values, so that we can treat people like objects—and, yes, abortion has helped us learn to do that; and an age of cracking the pillars of certainty—churches, schools, and political institutions—so that everything, including your life, my friend, is up for discussion... the methodical suffocation of authority and the hopeless balkanization of normative ethics. How delightful and endless our choices!—to kill, to die, to use until no longer useful, all without ever being judged, even by our selves. (Our *what?*) It is as Alisdair MacIntyre so aptly put it: The barbarians are *not* waiting beyond the frontiers; they have been governing us for some time.

I am one of those who helped usher in this barbaric age. I worked hard to make abortion legal, affordable, and available on demand. In 1968, I was one of the three founders of the National Abortion Rights Action League. I ran the largest abortion clinic in the United States, and as its director I oversaw tens of thousands of abortions. I have performed thousands myself. How could this have happened? How could I have done this? To understand, you must know something about my father and his gods.

In the past I did not feel fully able to tell this story. In 1979, when I published a semi-autobiographical book called *Aborting America,* my father, whom I loved deeply and loathed equally deeply, was still alive, and I suppressed many of my reminiscences, feelings, and memories in deference to my love, and my indebtedness to him. But this is 1996 (he died in 1990 at the Homeric age of ninety-four), and it is time to speak the whole truth: He was a formidable, dominant force in my life and in many ways forged the ruthless, nihilistic pagan attitudes and beliefs that finally drove me to unleash—with a handful of co-conspirators—the abortion monster.

My father was a remarkable man. He was born in New York City in 1895 to an immigrant German-Jewish pharmacist and his devoted German-Jewish immigrant wife. He was the last of four children of that union. Like most recent immigrants, the family lived in two rooms on the lower east side of Manhattan. My grandfather, the pharmacist, eked out a living helping the local apothecary while my grandmother took in sewing to supplement the bare-bones budget.

When my father was one year old, the pharmacist was afflicted with tuberculosis, in those days the most feared affliction imaginable, the AIDS of its time, and the extended family made a decision to send him to a sanitarium in Colorado. The working theory was that the pure fresh mountain air would so soothe the afflicted lungs that healing could then begin. But it was expensive to maintain him there, even though a number of aunts and uncles contributed their pittance to his upkeep each month (they were all recent immigrants and as impoverished as he). No social or medical safety nets then: It was work or starve. The pharmacist, who was not perceptibly improving at the sanitarium, somehow got word that his wife and children were in a state of near starvation, owing to the allocation of most of the available funds to his stay in Colorado; very shortly thereafter, he hanged himself in his closet, the better to divert the funds into food for his children. To his last conscious day my father would weep each time he told me this pitiful tale; of my sister's suicide (she was my only sibling) at the age of forty-nine he would not speak at all. She was divorced and had three children; no one ever divined a reason for her suicide. (In 1979, I could write these lines with the detachment of a Camus character; now I twist with pain and pray for the anodyne of prayer.)

The family then suffered a paralyzing fission: My grandmother was matched with a widower who lived in Ottawa, Canada. The widower was a *shochut,* the ritual slaughterer who would slaughter chickens and cows in the prescribed Old Testament manner so as to render them kosher. With five children of his own, he made it clear to my grandmother that he could accept only one of hers—the others would have to be placed with other members of the family, all of whom were as poor and laden with children as my grandmother, or placed in orphanages. A Sophie's Choice. She chose to bring little Joey, my father, then two years old, with her to Canada. The children left behind did indeed go to orphanages. They were, in their individual ways, scarred for life. So was my father.

Ottawa is the capital of Canada, but it was essentially a small one-business (government) town with a tiny Jewish community of perhaps fifty families. The community was so small and so poor—there was no work in the government for those exotic-looking Jews with their long black coats and beaver hats and *payesses* (the sideburns which are never to be cut and hang down, conspicuously curled, in front of the ears)—that it could not afford the upkeep of a rabbi. The *shochut,* then, was the reigning monarch of the Orthodox Jewish community and as such presided over weddings, funerals, bar mitzvahs, and the high holy days. Thus was my father raised in the most Orthodox Jewish community imaginable. It was said that when the founder of the Manischewitz Wine Company would take to the road to sell his product, he was such an observing Jew that he would never stay at a hotel, but would stay with the most Orthodox family in any community in which he happened to land that night. In Ottawa, that was my father's home. Such was the religious rigidity in which my father was raised.

He had the misfortune to be the brightest and the best of the six children in the household, and although he was the youngest, he was early singled out for training to enter that holiest of holy sodalities, the rabbinate. He attended Hebrew school daily. The curriculum was heavily weighted toward intensive analysis of the Talmud, thirty-five books of weighty words on the Jewish law. Toward the end of his life he would describe to me how he and his fellow *yeshivabuchers* (students of the Bible and Talmud) would spend hours on end in *pilpel,* hair-splitting discourse on the meaning of a single word in the Talmud. Torah and Talmud study would occupy his mornings; less pressing secular matters such as mathematics, Canadian history, French, and English literature would be presented to the semi-obtunded students after the lunch hour. At the age of thirteen he underwent the obligatory bar mitzvah: His most prized gift (gift-giving on this occasion dwarfed that of birthdays and Chanukah) was a pair of thick woolen socks his mother had knitted especially for him, to keep his feet warm during the frigid Canadian winter.

Then it was time to enter high school. There were two different paths a student could choose to follow at this juncture: the vocational high school—in which one would learn to be a mechanic, a bookkeeper, a farmer, and there was no tuition— or, if one were determined to pursue an academic future, Collegiate—a high school devoted to only secular studies. He had, from his earliest memory, a vocation: to be a doctor. Unfortunately, Collegiate was *not* free; one needed the tuition and the intelligence to enter Collegiate. The tuition was ten dollars annually. His stepfather, who was paid twenty-five cents for the kosher slaughtering of a chicken and fifty cents for bestowing the identical favor upon a cow, demurred; he could not afford the ten dollars, even though it meant that Joey would have to defer his dream of becoming a doctor to the indefinite future. No other relative would volunteer the money, and so Joey spent a distressing, frustrating year learning to be a bookkeeper. (After his death, as one of his executors, I went over his accounts and checkbooks: Although he died an extremely wealthy man, his financial record keeping was a fiasco. I doubt that the man ever troubled himself to balance his various checkbooks, keeping most of his financial records in his head.)

Ultimately, Joey's grandmother provided the necessary ten dollars each year in order for him to attend the Collegiate. He graduated with honors in that fateful year, 1914, was excused from service in the Canadian army during the First World War owing to his bad eyesight, and entered McGill University Medical College in the autumn of that year.

Still, he was grindingly poor. He trudged through the Montreal winters in a threadbare coat lined with newspapers; newspapers substituted for new soles in his shoes. His daily diet consisted of two slices of white bread and a cup of cocoa; on Saturday evenings he would splurge and have two eggs and two slices of toast at a restaurant on St. Catherine Street, the main drag of Montreal in that era. Within a year he developed a clinically recognizable case of hyponutrition: anemia (lack of sufficient red blood cells), hypoproteinemia (insufficient protein in his bloodstream to protect him from infection and to allow him to attain his genetically predetermined height), etc. The University Health Service recommended that he be discharged from school as physically unfit to carry out the demanding schedule and duties of a medical student although he was—at the end of his first year—ranked second in his class academically, surpassed only by a black man from the West Indies named

Philip Savory, who was working *his* way through McGill by performing the duties of a redcap at the Windsor train station in Montreal every night. Just as my father was about to be discharged, a kindly professor of medicine, who had taken a liking to this determined, plucky little fellow (he was five feet, four inches tall and weighed one hundred five pounds— including the wispy little mustache he affected), began asking him to his residence each Friday night, to eat with his family. He would fill up my father with huge slices of red meat, liver, and spinach; whatever was left over would be packed into a brown paper bag to take back to his room to be rationed out each night for the next week. Gradually his anemia improved, his proteins increased, and he even gained three pounds in the next year. In his later life, when he had become wildly successful beyond even his own dreams, he could never speak of Professor LaFleur without his eyes misting over. (He was the most soft-hearted and sentimental of men—and the most ruthless, unforgiving, hard-shelled operator imaginable. But more of *that* later.)

Something momentous overcame my father in his first year of medical school. In a growing disenchantment with the Judaic Orthodoxy that was brought on—according to him—by a liberal (no pun intended) dose of post-mature Enlightenment education, he rebelled against virtually all things Jewish at the end of his first year of medical school and broke his devoted mother's heart by renouncing the entire corpus of Jewish law, most importantly the dietary laws. He announced, not without an elegiac prelude, that henceforth (this adolescent mise-en-scène played itself out in the summer of 1915) he *would* mix meat and milk at the same meal; he *would* eat pork and pork products (the Sepoy mutiny in reverse); and he *would* eat seafood such as shrimp and lobster—and on and on, in a theatrical piece so poignant and juicy that it would have made Lawrence Olivier sick with envy. His justification of this earth-shattering religious volte-face was that in his first-year medical studies, he found not a shred of empirical evidence to support the constraints and restrictions imposed upon observing Orthodox Jews by the dietary laws. His mother wept bitter tears at his apostasy. Yet the truth is that he never ate pork products or seafood (two of the more unforgivable transgressions of the Talmud) until he watched *me* eat them when I was an adolescent: Not only was I not struck dead on the spot, but I actually seemed to be enjoying them. Henceforth, he ventured into that *goyische* swampland seemingly without a care—although on occasion, while he ate bacon with his eggs, I would note him furtively looking about with ears cocked, all antennae at the alert, the better I suppose to apprehend the sudden manifestation of the dreaded *moloch-hamovis* (angel of death). Like James Joyce he had renounced his religion, but it remained the hinge of his life and work all his days. No one, absolutely no one, could tell a Yiddish joke like my father; he would reduce rabbis to choking, quivering masses of jelly telling his jokes.

In his final (fifth) year of medical school (college and medical school were then combined into one entity) he met my mother. She was a tall, raw-boned, horsey woman, the eldest of six children born to John Dover, an Orthodox Jew and a wholesale dealer in farm produce: Sacks of potatoes were piled behind the couch in their parlor, and the family sat on crates of onions at mealtime. Needless to say, the family was as poor as my father's. Harriet Dover was three years older than Joey Nathanson—she was twenty-eight when he met her at a Jewish "social," and the family had already consigned her to spinsterhood. She was the eldest of six children and had dropped out of school in the sixth grade. What she and my father could have found in common to talk about, to laugh about, to romance about—that has eluded me all my adult life. Perhaps he was looking for another mother. Or perhaps I am indulging myself in pure psychobabble.

In any case, they became "engaged." Now, in the Jewish Orthodox community this is a very serious, generally irretrievable step—short of one or the other of the parties dying or committing suicide. It was also a financially complex and remarkably mercenary enterprise: The bride's father would sign a paper promising the groom a dowry, a substantial reward for having taken the unmarried daughter off his hands. In my mother's case, the agreed-upon sum was five hundred dollars, to be paid off within a year of the marriage.

My father had, upon finishing medical school, spent a year as an intern at the Ottawa Civic Hospital, then a leading medical teaching institution in the capital. He then took a residency training year at Bellevue Hospital in New York City. During that year, he tried desperately to break the engagement with my mother; she retaliated by threatening suicide and promising that the entire Jewish community in Ottawa would be apprised in painful detail of why she had taken her life, and who precisely was responsible for the act. It would create an irreparable *schande* (scandal), and any chance he would have to build a medical practice in that city would be doomed. Even his own mother and his stepfather, the *shochut,* whose opinions on matters of ethics and morality he valued, took offense at his attempts to end the relationship and counseled him accordingly.

In June of the following year, 1920, the wedding party assembled for the nuptials at the local (and only) synagogue. According to the negotiations, the first payment of the five-hundred-dollar dowry was due on the day of the wedding. My mother's father hurriedly mumbled something to the effect that in the hurly-burly of preparations he had forgotten to bring the money. My father, a profoundly suspicious man by nature, accused his prospective father-in-law of treachery, thievery, and welshing on his debt. It was only on the signing of another promissory note, witnessed by six of the guests at the wedding—three from the bride's side of the family and three from the groom's side, that the now-farcical but fatally poisoned ceremony went forward. Regrettably for her, my mother argued *her* father's position: that he was somewhat squeezed for cash at the moment but that John Dover was a man of his word and would honor his debts. This asseveration went wholly against the opinion of the tiny, almost incestuous community of Ottawa, which had it that the aforesaid John Dover was a thoroughgoing liar, a scoundrel, and a man sick with desperation trying to marry off his eldest child. That the object of his desperation was a promising, intelligent, young Jewish physician only quickened his pulses and stretched the already attenuated limits of his morality into the reaches of an einsteinian infinity.

My father had been counting on that dowry to finance a year in England training to be an ophthalmologist. When John Dover never made a single payment on the debt, my father was forced to abandon his ambitious plans to become a world-renowned eye doctor and instead had to settle for practicing general medicine for six years in the claustrophobic Ottawa Jewish community before heading south to the United States to specialize in obstetrics and gynecology in New York City in 1926.

My father never forgave my mother for her father's huggermuggery about the dowry. (Perversely, he kept all the relevant papers on this tragi-comedy and revealed them to me when I was fifty years old and he was in his eighties.) A vindictive, unforgiving man, he filed a lawsuit against his father-in-law months after he had married my mother, claiming to have been deceived, misled, and defrauded by Dover. The suit ripened, and several months later, on the eve of the trial, my mother revealed that she intended to testify on her father's behalf, denying that a dowry had ever been promised, and in fact if there were such a document attesting to the debt, it had been extracted under emotional duress from her father. Her sister Sylvia joined in the resistance. Fortunately a kindly, experienced trial judge persuaded my father to accept what seemed a reasonable compromise, that he would accept 50 percent of what he had been promised in exchange for dropping the suit. The case never came to trial, and my father commenced to nurture a towering hatred for my mother, her family—and Ottawa, Canada. He never forgave my mother; he would never allow her sister to enter his house, and on every appropriate (and some egregiously inappropriate) occasions, he would loudly curse the entire Dover lineage—and took especially perverse delight in doing so if my mother were present.

Why did he go through with the wedding in the first place? Why did he not divorce her after her shattering revelation that she was siding with her devious, lying father instead of her husband? My father had glib but transparently specious answers to these questions and others, such as why he had two children with this woman he hated so palpably. It is my conceit that despite his superficially brave apostasy from the constricting mores of the Jewish community in Ottawa, he was fearful of public opinion. Not persuaded? I have others: He was pathologically shackled to this woman three years older than him who perhaps represented, in his jumbled perception, his own devoted mother, who had rescued *him* from the orphanages; he was single-mindedly dedicated to the form of fathership, to somehow eradicate the lacerating pain of having been left fatherless himself at age two. And so on. And on. (How much psychobabble can you stand?) It remains that he fathered two children with Harriet Dover once they moved themselves to New York City, and that he was a fiercely protective, devoted, tyrannical, and ferociously just father who demanded unquestioning loyalty, submission, and uncritical partisanship.

CHAPTER 2

My Father's House

FROM MY EARLIEST MEMORIES, I am deeply disturbed by the pervasive repetitive paradoxes of my childhood: to be learned in Jewish matters, but not to worship. To be a respectful child, but only to him, the Strindbergian Father. My father traduced me from the age of six with histrionic tales of how my mother and my mother's family had bilked him, had coaxed and cajoled and promised him into a tragically sad and sorrowful marriage with a woman older, less intelligent, less erudite than he. We would take long walks together, he and I, and he would fill my ear with poisonous remarks and revanchist resolutions concerning my mother and her family. (Claudius filled the king's ear with no more lethal poison than my father filled mine.) My mother, aware of what he was doing, remained serene, civilized, and charitable—generous to a fault, despite my mindless parroting of the contumelies and insults that he had inculcated within me. I remained his weapon, his dummy, until I was almost seventeen years old when I—as he—rebelled and told him I would no longer function as his robotic surrogate assassin.

Almost as perverse as his orchestration of my relationship with my mother was his orchestration of my Judaism. Until my bar mitzvah he insisted on my attending *cheder* (Hebrew school) three times a week, in the afternoons after secular school, and he even required that I attend Sunday school at the local synagogue. When I came home from these excursions into the Jewish religion, he asked me what I had learned. And I would tell him, in a naive sort of way, since I was only nine or ten years old. Unfailingly, his reaction was to show his scorn for the teachings I had imbibed at his strict direction. At best, he showed a grudging tolerance for my recitation; more often, he derided me and laughed uproariously at what I had learned, then pulled apart with pointed questions the logic and substance of my lessons, undoubtedly the same questions he had asked himself some thirty years before when he made his apostasy. Not that I had built up an edifice of faith in my mind for him to destroy: there was far too much malice, strife, revanchism, and hate in the household in which I had been brought up.

In this world of psychological whipsaws and conflicting loyalties, I grew up with a first-class education. I attended the best private school in New York City from the age of eight. But my inner life was tumultuous, tortuous: no faith; no maternal love (I do not doubt that my mother doted on me and my sister, but she was a stiff, undemonstrative figure incapable of existing comfortably in the same room with the word "love"); and a veritable treasury of phobias, fantasies, and terrors. At age twelve I was convinced I was having a heart attack, and actually composed a last will and testament in which I left my baseball glove and basketball sneakers to my sister, Marion.

Marion: a sweet-natured innocent little child three years younger than I but, like me, captured and indoctrinated by my father with the same rancid swill directed at our mother. Marion was a bit of a tomboy and loved sports as did I, but the constant torrent of abuse against my mother led her to declare herself my father's dumb devoted ally, thus forsaking any chance at maternal love.

And so we grew, Marion becoming more and more magnetized to my father—even her gait came to resemble his; I more and more bitter, resentful, and worshipful of the man.

Rancor dominated our household. I recall with dismaying clarity that the dinner hour was always accompanied by a discussion of some current or historically relevant subject on which my father and I would disagree, often violently. The mother and the daughter usually fell silent during these disagreements, partly from ignorance and partly from a practiced deference. Furious to prove our points, we would rush to the library to pull the appropriate reference book (encyclopedia, usually) to resolve the argument. Invariably, of course, he was correct and I was wrong. (The motto under his picture in the yearbook of the graduating class at McGill University Medical College in 1919 read: "An insatiable thirst for knowledge.") In my now-yellowing tattered memories, there was never a discussion or disagreement on matters moral, ethical, or philosophical—it was always a date, a battle, a political issue, or a financial question.

Why do I recount this familial bilge to you? I will spare you the ineluctable tolstoian observation, but I implore you to consider the psychological abyss that yawned beneath me. Think of the insupportable confusion of a child growing up in this hate-filled household; think of the despair of an adolescent so thoroughly poisoned against his own innocent mother that he missed no opportunity to insult her, to denigrate her intelligence and her appearance—to the extent that one day after spewing a torrent of abuse at her and receiving surreptitious but approving glances from my father, she took a straight razor from his bathroom and chased me around the apartment with the avowed purpose of slashing my throat, the better to sever my vocal cords.

I had not a seedling of faith to nourish me. It is certainly true that I was inculcated with a certain antique Hippocratic morality. Profound respect was due to those who participated in one's education, and financial integrity was the keystone of the arch of morality. How many sermons, how many interminable lectures, did I sit through from my father on the evils of fee-splitting among doctors? How many self-serving encomia did I hear from him of how he had sturdily resisted the temptation to split fees? (Splitting fees was, simply put, the practice of a physician referring a patient to a specialist in another field and expecting a kickback from that specialist. Obviously, it encouraged dichotomy of interest, the benefit of which accrued only to the physicians involved, never to the patient, who was being bounced from one physician to another purely for monetary interest.)

But you may well ask, What does all this have to do with abortion? With experimentation on human embryos? With the perplexing issues of the use of fetal tissue for the treatment of adult disorders?

This: In the absence of any but the most crass instruction in interpersonal moral order, in the presence of a contempt for ethical relations with women, indeed for women themselves, in the expectation that I would blindly follow in the bloody footsteps of this warped and twisted man, a monster was germinating within me. The monster recognized nothing but utility, respected nothing but strength of purpose, craved love—and then perverted it.

You have every right to ask, What of your mother? Did she not instill in you any sound moral principles, any order of ethical decency? She was overpowered, as so many women of her generation were: unprotesting serfs and lackeys dwelling in an opulent seraglio, battening on mink coats, mah jong, and respectable maternity. She took no interest in my schoolwork (my father oversaw that aspect of my life with the zeal of an antebellum slave boss), and instead conducted every Friday night a pallid, watered-down version of the Shabbas service so brief and so apologetic (for the patriarch did not approve, and he had no hesitation in letting her know his sentiments during those five minutes or so, with his audible grunting and snuffling in the trough of food before him) as to be a caricature of a religious service. Poor woman, even in those five minutes she mouthed Hebrew prayers so inexpertly that I am convinced to this day that she had absolutely no knowledge of what it was she was praying for. Having lighted the candles on Friday night, she would lean over and brush my cheek with a kiss in the air, then dutifully plod to the other side of the table and do the same for my sister. She did not dare approach the patriarch.

My father, when he turned his back on Orthodox Judaism, was expressing *his* personal rebellion, his secularization. He had been brought up in tiny Ottawa, and a casual socializing with *goyim* (Gentiles) was beyond the Pale (the Pale of Settlement was an area of 386,000 square miles in czarist Russia in which the Jews were legally authorized to settle; by 1897 roughly five million Jews lived in this region bounded by the Baltic Sea and the Black Sea). At McGill University he met for the first time the *goyim* and discovered that not only were they hornless but that he could compete with them on equal terms intellectually and could even beat them at their own game. He was to be number two in his medical graduating class, edged out only by Philip Savory.

His rebelliousness expressed itself persistently all through his long life, but it was always filtered through the constricting prism of his early years of grinding poverty. He was unhesitating in the asseverations of racial equality, and in fact was the first obstetrician at the all-white, otherwise all-Gentile Woman's Hospital to insist that his black patients (referred to him by Philip Savory, who also found his way to New York City and massive wealth in the general practice of medicine in Harlem) be placed in semi-private rooms with white patients. He would explain it to me this way: "You see, son, they're in the same boat we are, i.e., discriminated against, so we must stick together." Not much of a rationale for upholding racial equality, but for his day it was a daring doctrine.

Or take his attitudes toward abortion. He was a stern patriarchal man for whom women were generally to be relegated to the back of the bus. Feminism was forty years away, and the rule (and more important, the law) was that no abortion could be done unless the life of the pregnant woman was in jeopardy. He spoke denigratingly of abortion and of abortionists. He had just enough of the Jewish respect for legal (and Hippocratic) authority that he would not flout the law. When I took the lead in the late 1960s in challenging those laws that restricted abortion, he professed disdain and shame for me. But near the end of his life he admitted to me that he had secretly admired me for my own rebelliousness and wished he had been part of that massive sexual revolution.

ALTHOUGH WE WERE BULLIED, my father did derive one of his great interests in life from something Marion said at the dinner table. It was a November evening in 1937 and Marion, then eight and a student at the fashionable Calhoun School in Manhattan, announced to the assembled that she had been assigned by her teacher a paper on Abraham Lincoln. With that, my father declared the usual moratorium on eating and rushed to the foyer of our apartment. The foyer (a quaintly elegant word one seldom sees any more in post-World War II boxy apartments economically partitioned to use every square inch of space for the necessities of living; the foyer with its proscenium entry into the living room was a pre-war luxury) contained massive shelves of books and at least four major encyclopedias, the jewel in the crown being the *Encyclopedia Britannica*. He pulled everything available on Abraham Lincoln, declared dinner a fait accompli, and proceeded to write—with very little contribution from my complaisant sister—her paper on the sixteenth president. Whether it was Lincoln's appearance, his humble origins, his strength of character, his undisputed affection for his children, his patently unhappy marriage—whatever it was (I am to this very day still puzzled over the intensity of the attraction he conceived for the martyred president), he formed a lifelong admiration for Lincoln, and acted upon it by prowling the book shops and curio places of dozens of cities in this country (and abroad), collecting books about Lincoln, icons of the man, copies of political cartoons of the era depicting Lincoln in a variety of forms, statuettes, and busts—in short, the foyer became a repository of what he liked to term *Lincolniana*. He became known throughout the nation as a scholar and collector of Lincoln memorabilia. He joined innumerable societies devoted to the study of Lincoln. He wrote several papers on rather obscure aspects of Lincoln's life, including one particularly intriguing one on Lincoln's relations with the Jewish community in the nineteenth century. (If this interests you, visit the Nathanson Collection on Abraham Lincoln at McGill University's new library, to which my father donated his entire collection.) Characteristically, my father never bought any Lincoln items that were truly rare: they were, he would say, "too rich for my blood." His early days of grinding poverty and his ubiquitous fear of a forced return to those unhappy circumstances demanded that he settle for second-level items, bits and pieces and likenesses that were interesting but not expensive. And so the collection (which grew progressively but in an orderly manner; he indexed and cross-referenced everything) is a superb research source for Canadian scholars of Lincoln but contained only one truly valuable item: the diary of the surgeon who cared for the president the night he was shot at Ford's Theater in April 1865.

Call it teenage rebelliousness, spitefulness, even jealousy, but I held myself aloof from the Lincoln fascination. Still, I did get the collecting bug from my father. He started it by assembling for me an album of cigar bands, those colorful labels put on cigars; until the Lincoln craze, he and I would go out on Saturday afternoons to prowl the cigar stores and persuade the owners to peruse their trash for old bands and donate them to us. We would then press them flat with an old-fashioned iron, mount them in our album, and admire the collection as it grew and prospered. Alas, I do not know where that collection is now, but I have been a collector since.

It was not until I was thirty that I found the writer who became for me what Lincoln was for my father. For my thirtieth birthday, my wife gave me a copy of Richard Ellman's biography of James Joyce, a writer whose work I had never read. She challenged me to read the work, and then I set out to read everything Joyce had written. Predictably, I became as fixated on Joyce as my father had been on Lincoln. I read everything he had ever written, obtained first editions of all his works, collected hundreds of books about Joyce, wrote scholarly papers on his work, and even taught courses on *Ulysses.*

Why did I become as fascinated with Joyce as my father had with Lincoln? No two men could have been more dissimilar. Lincoln was publicly agnostic and privately deeply religious, while Joyce was the archetypical lapsed and virulently anti-Catholic rebel. Lincoln embodied the virtues of the public servant: wisdom, integrity, mercy, wit, temperance, and strength—all dissolved in an attractive brew of existential melancholy and Platonic harmony. Joyce was a tumultuous, hard-drinking, half-blind Celt of colossal erudition and even more colossal egotism, contemptuous of the Irish, mankind, and God in equal draughts—yet Catholic to the marrow and fiercely Irish. More psychobabble perhaps, but Lincoln was the inexpressibly wise Old Testament Father-God for whom my poor father yearned all the days of his fatherless life; Joyce was the irreverent, passionate, disorderly genius that I have always admired, even revered. My father knew of my near-worship of Joyce and marveled frequently at the dimensions of my collection, but for the very life of him, he could never understand what I could see in such a dissolute, inharmonious, curmudgeonly misanthrope who turned out literature so patently incomprehensible that it defied even the *yeshivabucher* (student of the Talmud) in him.

My parents sent me to the Columbia Grammar School, one of the finest in New York. Columbia then had an overwhelmingly Jewish student body, the offspring of the most influential and wealthiest Jews in New York, such as Tom Sarnoff, son of General David Sarnoff, the founder and majority owner of NBC. The student body was probably 99 percent Jewish. I remember only one boy in our class of thirty-two who wasn't Jewish. He was Tom Mix, a tall, thin, gangling, and remarkably pale young man to whom I had taken a liking; I would invite him over to our house for games after school or on Saturdays. (I think the current parlance is "play dates.") I was vaguely aware that he wasn't Jewish, but the subject never arose until one day when I, now nearing eleven years of age, and several other Jewish boys fell to discussing our plans for attending the Passover seder. When it came Tom's time to speak, he almost apologetically blurted out that he was "Gentile" and didn't celebrate such holidays. An awkward silence settled over the group and, perhaps for the first time in my young life, I realized that there were those who did not share the *yiddishkeit* or that easy sense of community Jews enjoy in each other's company and about which Irving Howe wrote so eloquently in *World of Our Fathers.* It meant the easy trading of mutual experiences (What Hebrew school do you go to? Are your parents Orthodox, Conservative, or Reform? Do you keep kosher?), the occasional injection of a Yiddish expression, and the shared eager anticipation of the flood of gifts to come with the bar mitzvah at thirteen. Tom Mix, I suddenly realized, was an alien in this world. From that day on my relations with him were never again easy.

Although the student body was overwhelmingly Jewish, the teaching staff was almost entirely non-Jewish. The headmaster, a distinguished-looking graduate of Dartmouth University named Mr. Alden, was careful to eschew any references to religion. Nevertheless, at Christmas we sang Christmas carols in Latin, and from time to time the teachers would lead us in the

Lord's Prayer. I truly believe that those Christmas carols, the Christmas decorations, and the trees at school benevolently flavored my early life. Even then, I dimly perceived that Jesus Christ was not a demon. I was vaguely aware that the One responsible for such incredible beauty must have *some* redeeming qualities.

My father, as I have already noted, had turned against religion, and I believed that religion had nothing to give me, that it was a millstone. Still, I continued to attend Hebrew school three times weekly until I was bar mitzvahed. At my father's insistence, Columbia Grammar School had arranged for a teacher to shuttle me over to the Hebrew school after classes were finished for the day at Columbia. The Hebrew school was located in the back of the V'nai Jeshurun synagogue, on Broadway and Eighty-ninth. It was a "Conservative" congregation, neither Orthodox nor Reformed but heavily tilted toward Orthodoxy and relegating the women to a curtained balcony. We had two teachers. One was Lewis Terman, a stern, reedy rodent of a man with an ominous pencil-thin mustache, and the other was his warm, endearing wife, whose lovely manners and kindly interest in us never flagged. How could I have forgotten the name of one so dear?

Mr. Terman, on the other hand, was a brute. The rumor was that he urinated icicles; I saw no reason to doubt this. His main concern seemed to be how fast we could read the various prayers in Hebrew, and twice a week he would stage contests involving speed. I inevitably placed second to a boy named Burt, who seemed able to reel off vast chunks of the Siddur (prayer book) at a velocity that would have made Evelyn Wood reel in amazement. What did the prayers mean? How did they translate into English? Such peripheral considerations were not deemed important in Mr. Terman's fast-paced classes. We were insulted and punished with extra work if we fell behind. For many years, Mr. Terman epitomized for me the Jewish religion: stern, unforgiving, and alienating. Sunday school was no better. Bored, arrogant teachers taught us Jewish history as names, dates, battles, and dusty tales of talmudic scholars and prosperous heroes.

It is not my purpose here to present myself as victim: I am sure that many a Catholic recalling his childhood religious training could with no difficulty recite the same litany of complaints about the catechisms and the memorializing of the days of the saints, but in the center of my particular torment there was a great aching void.

My childhood image of God was—as I reflect on it six decades later—the brooding, majestic, full-bearded figure of Michelangelo's Moses. He sits slumped on what appears to be his throne, pondering my fate and at the brink of disgorging his inevitably damning judgment. This was my Jewish God: massive, leonine, and forbidding.

(What a revelation for me when in the United States Air Force, out of sheer frustration and boredom, I began attending an evening course in Bible study and discovered that the New Testament God was a loving, forgiving, incomparably cosseting figure in whom I would seek, and ultimately find, the forgiveness I have pursued so hopelessly, for so long.)

Of course, while we were not religious, we did celebrate the Jewish holidays to their fullest. For the Jewish high holy days (Rosh Hashanah, Yom Kippur), my father would dutifully purchase tickets for my mother and him to attend the services. As a child, I naively assumed that all religions demanded tickets for attendance at ceremonial occasions, much like going to football game's. (Even at the tender age of nine I was a devoted fan of the New York Giants baseball and football teams.) It was not until I reached my middle teens—several years after my bar mitzvah at age thirteen, after which I never set foot in a synagogue again—that I commenced to wonder why it was that the Jewish religion required the purchase of tickets for the purpose of worship whereas other religions had an open-door policy. I was aware that a collection plate was passed around at the appropriate time in Roman Catholic and Protestant services, but ticket-buying for this purpose smacked of regarding religion as an entertainment—or worse, a commodity of some indefinable sort. To this day I am still astonished that the practice continues unabated, and have actually witnessed ticket scalpers hawking scarce Yom Kippur ducats on Fifth Avenue just outside the doors of the Temple Emanuel. What sort of religion is it that one has to buy one's way into the house of worship in order to commune with God? I am to this day bemused by this bizarre practice. I do not doubt that it has contributed, if only marginally, to my apostasy.

My father would attend the services on those high holy days and, having been trained to the rabbinate, he would not only chant along with the cantor and pray along with the rabbi, but he would also sway along with the congregation (Jews sway back and forth while they pray; there is a rough correlation between the angle of sway and the degree of one's religious ardor, but that may be Nathanson's law and not verifiable in any reliable statistical manner). The youngsters like myself would take a break every so often and leave the *shul* (synagogue) for a short time to chat with friends on the sidewalk outside, tease girls, and giggle over some elderly Jew who—in a fit of religious fervor—had chanted louder than the rest of the congregation, belched (anathema on Yom Kippur, a day of strict fasting), or been flatulent during a particularly solemn moment in the service.

The holy days were almost always in September, usually in the Indian summertime, and we young boys would have been thrust into our Sunday-best clothes; this was a time long before the development of lightweight fabrics, and I would perspire profusely in my navy wool suit and my bogartian gray fedora. I was so sensitive to the rough wool, made even more distasteful by the sweat soaking it, that I took to wearing a pair of light play trousers *under* my navy wool trousers. My parents thought this practice hilarious and never missed an opportunity to remind me that a rip or tear in my pants would be an insignificant event since I had another pair beneath them—a spare pair, they called it. The revelation—that they knew of this practice and derided it—was an endless source of embarrassment to me, though not so embarrassing that I would abandon the practice.

After the Yom Kippur services, which generally broke about five in the afternoon (I had manfully fasted all day on that holy day since the age of eight), we would all repair to my parents' apartment on West Eighty-sixth Street near Central Park. There uncles, aunts, friends, and acquaintances would gather (my mother's family was *not* permitted) to feast. We would always begin with pitchers of orange juice (my father the doctor prescribed this for everyone, on the sound physiologic rationale that this would raise the depleted blood sugar faster than anything else) and then all the traditional dishes would spew forth from the kitchen (cooked largely by the black maid, a much superior cook to my mother, whose only culinary expertise was in the creation of good pastries, especially a light and mouth-watering cheesecake): the stuffed derma (a heavy concoction of dough and lard, liberally doused with a tasty brown gravy); gefilte fish (a brutalized version of quenelle made with the ground flesh of the carp and the pike); matzo ball soup (chicken soup with scattered boulders of cornmeal); kasha varnishkes (ravioli-like sculptures stuffed with buckwheat and flooded with the same heavy, delicious gravy that had drowned the stuffed derma); lox (as opposed to "smoked salmon"—it was thicker, richer, and much more greasy and fatty); great platters of sour cream, cottage cheese, and cream cheese, and huge loaves of challah, the yellow eggy bread with the convolutions and gyri on the top of the loaf.

After everyone had been sated; after all the reaching, mumbling, gobbling, and the swilling of the cloyingly sweet Manischewitz ceremonial wine; after the obligatory trips to the bathroom and then to the living room couches to lie down and "let the food settle," the leaden troops would rally and gather yet again at the mammoth dining table for the customary poker game. My father was a shrewd and invariably successful player, but my poor mother, who was an expert bridge player, was no match for the vultures who regarded the poker game with the same reverence that a riverboat gambler would. Amid screams, dissatisfied rumbles, curses, and imprecations, the game would finally break up at ten or eleven in the evening, and my sister and I (having long since excused ourselves at my father's direction to do homework and then go to bed) would hear the slamming of the doors, the slurred vows to repeat the performance next year ("God willing"), and the whine of the ancient elevator as it bore the worshipers, the gourmands, and the cardsharps to the ground floor where the metallic crash of the elevator gates being drawn back would mark the end of the holiday.

Where was God in all this commerce, this revelry, this gambling and cursing and lurching out the door? Had he been there at the table watching us, watching me build my "Dagwood sandwiches" (a slice of challah, some chunks of tomato, lettuce, cream cheese, gefilte fish, stuffed derma, hard-boiled eggs, another enclosing slice of challah)? The building and wolfing of these sandwiches always amused the relatives and friends, and my father would nod approvingly. The sense of community was overpowering, but I can to this very day feel the void, the hollow center of all the celebration and good feeling: What indeed were we celebrating? It seemed to me then, and the intuition persists, that we were all celebrating the *end* of the fast, the getting through of another high holy day. It was more a rite of passage than a religious observation, and I came away from it with the satisfied air of a survivor, not feeling that I was one of God's creatures who had confessed my sins to Him (Yom Kippur is a Day of Atonement, a day in the year set aside to acknowledge one's trespasses and transgressions) and had received absolution—and I suspect the others felt the same.

THE EPICENTER OF MY FANTASY WORLD, the nucleus of my imagination, was the cinema. The black-and-white medium was itself a representation of certainty. The plots were predictable and ecstatically moral. The actors were certain: Gary Cooper was always a hero, Edward Arnold a dependable villain, and Madeline Carroll, Norma Shearer, Paulette Goddard, and Carole Landis were all beautiful, charming, and exquisitely desirable. To enter a movie house was to enter a universe as certain and as believable for me as a church was for a devout Catholic. The pillars were cracking around us in the thirties, but good old Hollywood reassured us of the timeless certainties, with all the perplexing questions, the discomforting sexuality, and the undefined quiddities strained out. What was left was an infinitely soft puree of life.

The movie house above all was a refuge from the tumultuous parody of a marriage, in the vortex of which my sister and I lived. A magazine, *Movie Story,* was the map of my refuge. It did *not* review films but gave a detailed list of the cast of characters, summarized the plots with considerable detail, and, most important, gave the exact running time of each movie. Now this may seem a small thing to the reader but to Bernard, age twelve and yearning for a safe dark place in which to lose himself, this was a critical matter. Errol Flynn movies generally ran long, and I recall reading once of one of his films that ran more than two hours. In those days the double feature was the standard, so, combined with the inevitable B film that accompanied the Flynn feature, I could count on a solid three hours of ecstatically squinching down in my seat and smiling in the dark.

I went alone to the movies—not even my sister could accompany me, unless by paternal fiat. I always sat in the second or third row, the better to lose myself in the screen universe. A yawning hole in the middle of me, filled once a week with chiaroscuro fantasy, cheap imitations of life, made-in-Taiwan trinkets. Belief wafer-thin, faith utterly absent. Running on duty (my first duty was to my duty), paternal authority, a farrago of obligation, pride, and an existential anxiety so powerful as to drive me panic-stricken to every visible exit except the one most obvious: faith and belief. That had been barred to me and was no longer even visible.

BY NOW IT SHOULD BE UNMISTAKABLY clear to the reader that the center of my universe was my father; my mother had long since become, for me, a wraith. I spoke of the omnipresent psychological whipsaws in which I grew up: no consistent normative morality, no ethical rules applicable to the good life. To be sure, my father insisted on absolute honesty in my dealings with him and society (although he had no reluctance to lie brazenly to my mother concerning his extramarital sexual activities and encouraged me implicitly to do likewise). The only time he ever struck me was when he caught me in a foolish little lie at age eleven involving my solemn promise to him not to stop and pick up a friend on the way to Sunday school. Of course I did; he discovered me in flagrante delicto, waiting for my friend to come downstairs to go to Sunday school, and he struck me across the mouth, proclaiming my mendacity and warning me that I should never lie to *him*. He often trumpeted to me that "one lie leads to another," but never spoke to the immorality of lying.

He himself was, to the end, a deeply confused, fragile, driven man with no point to his life: He relished the accumulation of wealth, but never spent a penny more than he absolutely had to. He revered (and practiced) learning but never dared plunge below the surface facts and figures to explore the whys and the why nots. He considered himself a rebel and an innovator, but retained all his life a mordant fear of authority (he would always overpay his taxes, in the fear that the IRS might one day show up on his doorstep and demand an accounting). The awareness of a policeman's gaze upon him would turn him to jelly even though he had done nothing outwardly wrong.

He did not believe in God, but in some "superior power." All his life he proclaimed that he wanted nothing to do with primitive rituals like funerals but wished merely to be cremated in the most efficient and least ceremonial manner. But his will stipulated that he be buried alongside his star-crossed daughter, whom he had reduced to less than a cipher in his lifetime. I, as his only immediate heir and survivor, honored his wish, although in the first hours after his death I arranged for the cremation he had supposedly sought, and was thunderstruck when his granddaughter, my late sister's daughter, produced a document verifying that he had bought a burial plot next to my sister's immediately after her death, and had planned to be buried alongside her—despite the surface rodomontade of cremation, efficiency, and lack of ceremony.

If anything, my sister was even more dominated by our father than I was. In falling completely under his spell, Marion had become nearly invisible. She parroted his words and clothed herself in his frequently irrational attitudes. (He had conceived an almost psychotic detestation of Franklin Roosevelt, and to hear the words of hate for FDR spilling out of her innocent mouth was an experience at first ludicrous but increasingly pathetic.) She ceded her entire life to our father.

When it was time to marry after she was graduated from college in Boston, my father picked the prospective groom, cajoled him with promises of financial help (the fiancé was a dentist), and ultimately engineered the marriage; there were three children of the union—which lasted until Arnold (the husband and father) declared himself independent of my father on one stormy Sunday afternoon on a Thanksgiving day weekend (he had by now a flourishing dental practice), and my father decreed that it was time to dissolve the marriage—that *he* would care for Marion and her three children. Dutifully, she divorced Arnold, gave up her large and lavish home in Yonkers for a boxy ground-floor apartment in Riverdale, and lived thereafter on the pitifully small dole my father would hand to her each month with all the ceremony of the ransoming of a monarch.

Her mental health destroyed, her physical health intact but—
to her befuddled mind—suspect, her children rebellious, fallen
in with bad company, and truant, my sister killed herself one
sunny August morning with an overdose of a powerful sedative.
Her children discovered her early that morning, the body half
in and half out of bed, the bottle of pills empty. They called my
father, who rushed to her apartment, sobbed uncontrollably for
an hour, and then (in clear defiance of the law in these matters)
represented himself as her personal physician, signed her death
certificate with a fiction centering on heart disease, and had her
buried within twenty-four hours. The burden of yet another
suicide of someone close to him was evidently unbearable. He
was eighty-four years old when she died (she was forty-nine),
and for the rest of his life he never spoke of her death. With the
mention of her name, he would break into a long, gasping, gut-
teral keening, a sound so fearfully animal that it would provoke
a disbelieving shudder in anyone who heard it.

And I? I have had three failed marriages and have fathered a
son who is sullen, suspicious but brilliant in computer science.

CHAPTER 3

The Pillar of Fire

I BEGAN COLLEGE IN THE SUMMER of 1943. World War II was moving to a crescendo on both fronts, and I entered college with a lingering sense of exclusion from that drama. The campus at Cornell was swarming with students from the armed forces, and the young *descamisados* generally felt like pariahs, especially if suffering from no obvious disabling affliction. My roommate, Joe Nemeth, who had polio as a child and could barely hobble from class to class, was immune from what I perceived to be the accusatory stares of the uniformed.

How I longed to be in the Army, to be a part of the Armageddon taking place across the globe! When I turned eighteen in the beginning of my second year at Cornell (we were on an accelerated program, and by that time I had acquired enough credits to qualify as a junior), I was summoned to appear for a military physical. I was thrilled at the prospect of being drafted and dutifully informed my father that I had gotten my "greetings" letter from Uncle Sam.

To this day I do not know how he accomplished it. Did he know someone on my local draft board? Did he attest I suffered from some mythical disease? Somehow or other I was examined, pronounced unfit for military service because my eyesight was defective, and deferred as a 4-F, to continue my premedical studies at Cornell. I was moderately nearsighted. Arthur Sloane, a classmate of mine at Columbia Grammar School with the same minor affliction, was drafted when we were graduated from high school and was killed in action in the Battle of the Bulge.

In later years my father and I never discussed that episode. I quite simply did not want to hear the truth. I believe that, in his unquenchable zeal to have me become a physician and follow in his illustrious footsteps, he transgressed some indefinable moral, perhaps even legal, standard. It would have been unbearably embarrassing for us both to reopen that sore. Suffice it to say that I resented his interference then, and even now I find it difficult to understand such an uncontrollable infringement on my autonomy. But then, as Pascal once said, "The heart has its reasons, of which reason knows nothing," and I (charitably, I believe) attribute his thwarting of my wish to go to war as the manifestation of a man deeply attached to his only son, determined to spare his son the grim realities of war and even more bent on casting his son into the physician mold he himself had lusted after so indomitably.

I pursued my studies at Cornell with middling success; I was summoned to the office of the dean of liberal arts once to explain why I had been systematically cheating another younger roommate in our nightly poker game. (I never cheated him; he complained to his mother that he was losing all his allowance money in the game, and the truth is he was an appallingly bad poker player.) I remained an independent, never joined a fraternity, and had few friends. My father, I believe, preferred it this way, the better to concentrate on my studies and gain rapid admission to medical school. The few friends I had were New York Jews of less affluent upbringing and for the most part inclined strongly to the politics of the radical Left, e.g., the Young Communist League, then known as the American Youth for Democracy. A political virgin, I went to a few meetings of this group, found myself unutterably bored (and the coeds attending those meetings were uniformly humorless, heavily mustached, and as swarthy as gypsies), and quickly surrendered whatever fledgling interest I had nourished in that realm. But that transient and seemingly innocent episode returned to haunt me in the McCarthy era.

My father had the cunning to cultivate artfully the favor of one F. Cyril James, the principal (read president) of McGill University in the mid-forties. James was a suave, creaseless Englishman who would best be played by the venerable C. Aubrey Smith if one were casting a movie of his life. He was also a drinker of colossal capacity, while my father had no experience with alcohol save for the cloyingly sweet wines of the various Jewish high holy days. When James visited New York, my father would take him to dinner and try to match him drink for drink at the Yale Club; inevitably, the taxi would pull up in front of our apartment house on Eighty-sixth Street at 8 P.M., and my father would stagger out and puke his guts in the street: he'd had another heart-to-heart chat with F. Cyril James. These chats were to serve me in good stead.

When it came time for me to apply for admission to medical school, I was directed by my father to apply at only two institutions: Harvard and McGill. I was rejected at Harvard. I did not mourn the rejection at Harvard, but when I received a letter of rejection from McGill I was truly astonished. My father had assured me that admission to McGill Medical School was as certain as the planets in their orbits. I telephoned to give him the news on a Friday morning in mid-April 1945. I could sense the suffusion of blood coursing to his face in the wake of the news. He fumed a few moments, promised me I would be in McGill come September, and abruptly hung up. Four days later I received an apologetic note from Principal James that there had been an inexcusable error at the secretarial level in the office of the dean of the medical school, and of course I was to report to the medical school on September 1, 1945.

Many years later my father related to me his subsequent conversation with James that fateful day, chuckling when he told me that he had known exactly when to call the principal, out of a profound knowledge of the man's drinking habits, and had protested to him of the palpable injustice ongoing in excluding his son from the entering medical class at McGill. James instantly sat down to draft a note to the dean of the medical school and had it delivered by messenger to all concerned with the admission process; before his headache had ebbed the following morning, I was in the entering class.

MY SAGA TRULY COMMENCES HERE: a hot, humid Indian summer day in Montreal, Canada, the day on which I registered for my first-year medical classes. The medical school then was located in Strathcona Hall, a medieval castle with formidable gray stone walls, vast arches framing heavy doors, and cone-shaped battlements at the corners of the building. Lining the walls of the interior were plaques commemorating the reigns of various faculty members. The names were all too familiar to me: Henry

LaFleur, Sir William Osler, Walter Chipman—these were the heroes of the stories of my childhood and adolescence. My father had saturated me with the virtue, the wisdom, and the dedication of these men. Expectation pressed in on me with crushing force; how to live up to his sterling record achieved in the face of unspeakable adversity. Still, it was a moment of indescribably sweet solemnity.

I lived then in a cavernous rented room on University Street, two blocks from the medical school. My landlady was an obese, neurotic dervish of a woman named Eva Long, who had perfected a noiseless walk that would put Sitting Bull to shame: She would sneak up to my door at odd hours, then knock boldly and announce that it was too late for pacing the room/keeping lights on for studying/entertaining classmates with whom I was reviewing material for examinations. My rent was ten dollars per week, payable a month in advance.

That first year I took my breakfast and supper at a boarding house around the corner from my room. The proprietress was a beefy, hearty Scottish woman who delighted in seating twelve of us medical students at a baronial table in the middle of the dining room, then throwing down giant haunches of steer, vats of mashed potatoes, heaping mounds of brussel sprouts (why do the Scots love brussel sprouts so?); her pièce de résistance was the Sunday lunch (in lieu of supper that day), which consisted of tubs of barley soup, rare roast beef sliced so thin it was virtually translucent, and brussel sprouts. It was family-style but with a well-established pecking order: The most senior students sat at the head of the table, the most junior ranged along the flanks. There was always enough to eat, but the Scottish woman (where is her name?) was a bear for punctuality, and if one were three minutes late, the doors would be irrevocably shut for that meal.

I doled out forty dollars a month for the boarding house. Since my father had me on a budget of ninety dollars a month, this left me with very little extra to spend on luxuries such as newspapers, cigarettes, and what my father would term "incidentals." I smoked a pack a day in medical school; the professor of pathology, Dr. Lyman Duff, smoked three packs a day and even then, during lectures, was inveighing against cigarettes as the cause of lung cancer. The poor man died of lung cancer not long after I graduated from school in 1949. Not exactly a lucullan existence, but compared with my father's ordeal it was tolerable enough.

Human memory is a kind and reliable device. I recall my classes that first year with a crystalline clarity. Anatomy was taught by an Irish scholar, Dr. John Martin, who wore a black headband at all times: I was told that the back portion of the headband (which was fusiform) concealed a bullet hole in his skull that he had never bothered to have repaired; he was reputed to have been a Sinn Fein hothead in his early years, and had been shot in the head by the Black and Tans who occupied Ireland in the times of the "troubles." Notwithstanding, he was a superb teacher: colorful, playful, learned, and inspiring. Hebbel Hoff was my physiology professor: sardonic, effete, and not a little cruel. Blondish wavy hair framed a pudgy boyish face but concealed a ruthless insatiable ego; I learned comparatively little from this man. My classmates detested him as much as did I.

The shining faculty light of that first year was Dr. David Thompson, a thin, reedy figure with the face of an English general, guardsman's mustache and all, and the manners of a perfect gentleman. He taught us biochemistry in such an orderly, refined, and elegant manner that to this day I can still recall the substance of many of his lectures. I had never enjoyed chemistry at Cornell, but Thompson brought it to life for me. He always had time for questions afterward, and even the most ludicrous question was treated with a respectful gravity. He was perhaps the most revered member of the McGill medical faculty, and deservedly so.

One professor, however, made a greater impression on me than any other, far greater than I understood at the time. The professor was a man named Karl Stern, a profoundly erudite psychiatrist who was, in the McGill professorial galaxy, a star among stars. He was born at the turn of the twentieth century in a small Bavarian town near the Bohemian border into a Jewish family that appears to have been of a Conservative stripe: neither strictly Orthodox nor liberally Reform. (The ancient joke goes that Reform Jews are so liberal that their synagogues are closed for the Jewish holidays.) Stern was educated in Germany, where he obtained a medical degree. While in college, he committed himself to Orthodox Jewry for a brief period of time. He scrupulously observed the dietetic laws, studied Hebrew, and even donned the *t'fillen* during morning prayer. *T'fillen* are little leather boxes that contain slips of parchment upon which are imprinted passages from the Exodus and Deuteronomy Books of Moses. The boxes are worn by Orthodox Jews on the head and left arm daily except for the Sabbath and the high holy days to remind them of their sacred prayer duties as set forth in the Mishneh Talmud. There is a story that circulates among Orthodox Jews (my father's legacy to me, in part) which goes like this:

A Gentile patient in the hospital receives as his roommate an Orthodox Jew, who has an unspecified ailment. On their first morning together, the Orthodox Jew begins wrapping the *t'fillen* around his left arm, soundlessly. The Gentile observes the procedure, rolls his eyes heavenward, and blurts out: "Those Jews. So smart. Only a few hours in the hospital, and already he's taking his own blood pressure."

Stern's retreat into the religious fortress was no accident. Although he failed to find the comfort he sought so intensely in the anfractuous, often enigmatic, warrens of the Jewish faith, he was later to seek—and find—that pillar of fire in another era, half a world away.

My first encounter with Stern was in 1948, my fourth year of medical school. He was then second in command at the Allen Memorial Institute, the psychiatric teaching hospital of McGill. He reported only to Dr. D. Ewen Cameron, a benign but rather flatulent psychiatrist who had traded on his fame as one of the psychiatric panel members at the Nuremberg trials to become professor and chairman of psychiatry at McGill after the Second World War. However, all of us students knew that while Cameron was able and affable, Stern was the dominant figure in the department: a great teacher; a riveting, even eloquent lecturer in a language not his own; and a brilliant contrarian spewing out original and daring ideas as reliably as Old Faithful. I conceived an epic case of hero-worship for Stern, read my psychiatry with the diligence of a biblical scholar, and in turn was awarded the prize in psychiatry at the end of my fourth year. Stern even hinted to me that an application from me for the coveted residency in psychiatry at Allen Memorial would not be looked on with disfavor; i.e., just let us know you're interested, you idiot, and we'll make a special place for you in our program. Regretfully, I declined the offer, resolving instead to move ahead into residency programs aimed at obstetrics and gynecology.

The reader may wonder why I dwell on Stern. There was something indefinably serene and certain about him. I did not know then that in 1943—after years of contemplating, reading, and analyzing—he had converted to Roman Catholicism. It was not until 1951 that he published his book, *The Pillar of Fire,* perhaps the most eloquent and persuasive document on the experience and dynamics of religious conversion written in the modern age. It was a selection of the Catholic Book Club and also of the Thomas More Book Club in that year. In it, he did what perhaps only a few (Maimonides, Mendelssohn, Spinoza) had done: reconciled truth in religion with aristotelian empirical science.

In the last section of his book, which he entitled "Letter to my Brother," he explained to his brother, an observing Jew who had survived the Holocaust, why he had converted to Catholicism, and how science and religion coexist:

> The Church is immutable in her teaching. There is only one supernatural truth, as there is only one scientific truth. That in the mastering of matter constitutes the law of Progress, in things of the spirit is the law of Preservation. I remember when I showed you the Papal encyclical about the Nazis. You were quite impressed, and you said: "This sounds as if it had been written in the first century." That's just the point!

In this extraordinary document, he asks the question that has dogged me for too many years. He puts the question to his brother this way:

> Now perhaps you will say: "How can you, as an educated person...?" or "How can you, as a man with

scientific training...?" or "How can you, with knowledge of psychoanalysis...?" There seem to be a great
number of How Can You questions. In all sincerity I
do not even understand why these questions are asked.

He goes on to answer these pointless conundra in a manner as
simple as a child's, as sophisticated as a world-renowned psychiatrist, as humble as the most faithful Servant of God. But the
answer that captivated me was the one I had been searching for,
the one that answers the How-Can-You-as-a-Scientist question; he says:

> Some time ago I read in a German history of
> Philosophy that Pascal's early death was caused by the
> inner tortures he endured resulting from the conflict
> between Science and Religion. It is quite possible that
> Pascal suffered inner conflicts, but there is no indica-
> tion that this was one of them. I presume that
> DeBroglie is a Christian, and that [Max] Planck was a
> Christian. Pascal and Newton were Christians. It is
> possible that they were Christian *besides* being scien-
> tists, or on *account* of being scientists, but why should
> they have been Christians *in spite of* being scientists?

Stern and I, during my last year at McGill, forged a strong, even
compelling teacher–student relationship. I embraced every word
that came out of his mouth, not primarily on the prima facie
scientific substance but because of the serenity and the certainty
with which he spoke. It was not the scholastic hubris of other
professors, but the warm comfort of an ageless wisdom with
which he expressed himself. Remember, this was 1949, I had

absolutely no knowledge of his conversion, and we never discussed religion. It came as a shock to me to pick up a tattered paperback copy of his book in 1974 when I was floundering in the wake of my hegemony of the abortion clinic and the doubts that were beginning to crack my own pillars of certainty, to discover that even as I had spoken to him on so many occasions about so many other things, he possessed a secret I had been searching for all my life—the secret of the peace of Christ.

Karl Stern and I encountered each other twice, with twenty-five years between the encounters; the second encounter launched my search for spiritual truth. Only the Hand of God could have engineered such a ratifying experience as this.

CHAPTER 4

The Story of Ruth

McGill University was founded by a Scot, James McGill, and leaned heavily upon British theories and practices of pedagogy: virtue and even a strong tradition of self-denial in the teacher, and absolute obedience on the part of the student; a reliance on brute memory out of proportion to reasoned dialogue with the student; and always a distance (taking on the shape of a caesarean hauteur) on the part of the professor.

In the medical school, these practices generally prevailed, though less rigidly than they had in my father's day.

But this relationship between student and teacher was less essential to my story than that of physician to patient. The Hippocratic tradition—with its emphasis on the reverence to be accorded one's teachers, the implied exclusivity of the medical sodality, even a quasi secrecy regarding the healing arts, encouraged the ideal of the domination of the patient by the virtuous and paternalistic physician. The patient had little or nothing to say regarding treatment, and even to question the doctor on these matters was regarded as heresy. Today's concepts of second opinions, informed consent, and the moral and ethical duties would have been inconceivable in Montreal in those years.

This paternalistic tradition assumed, however, not only a high degree of personal virtue in the physician but his commitment to an acknowledged ethical code. The Hippocratic Oath states the following:

> I will give no deadly medicine to anyone if asked, nor suggest any such counsel; and in like manner, I will not give to a woman a pessary [a device inserted in the vagina, thought erroneously to initiate an abortion] to produce an abortion.

The oath is unambiguous on these matters. To bulwark these strictures, we had several lectures in obstetrics and gynecology in my third year of medical school in which the dangers (legal as well as medical) of induced abortion were drilled into us— although there were at least three abortionists with flourishing practices working in Montreal at that time, protected from the middling corrupt police department by modest levels of bribery.

I recall an occasion on which I saw a woman, bleeding profusely and in excruciating pain, being brought up to the gynecology ward of the Royal Victoria Hospital (the prestigious teaching hospital of the McGill University Medical School). She was lying on a gurney wheeled by an orderly and surrounded by two policemen and one resident physician; I (the student) trailed in their wake. Once she was placed in bed the minions of the law took over, elbowing the physicians aside and interrogating her about her miscarriage, obviously convinced that she had had an illegal induced abortion. The interrogation went on for fifteen minutes during which time I stood transfixed (I was in my third year at the time). How could police matters take precedence over the care of this poor soul in pain? And the grim, avenging visages of the two policemen—it was as if they had personally been assaulted—have stayed with me vividly these many years. It was not until they had finished their inquisition that the physician was allowed to minister to the patient. Ironically, Montreal is now a center for abortion in Canada, courtesy of the notorious Henry Morgenthaler, whose abortion clinics sprawl across the Canadian map like so many fast food franchises.

As to the prohibition on giving "deadly medicine" (euthanasia), I recall well the knowing winks and nudges of the residents in pediatrics when we made our nursery rounds in my fourth year and inquired about the mongoloid child that had been admitted to the nursery the day before, only to be counted among the missing today. Hypocritical Hippocratic medicine, at the whim of the imperial physician.

The original oath was written two thousand five hundred years ago. The second part of the oath, which treats of deadly medicine and abortion, appears to have reflected the ideas of the pythagorean sect rather than the general attitudes of the ancient Greek physician, although Galen—Hippocrates' most illustrious descendent in ancient medicine—seems to have practiced in congruence with all the tenets. The remarkable longevity of the oath is probably accounted for by its compatibility with Christianity. There is said to be a Christian version of the Hippocratic Oath, written in the tenth or eleventh century, entitled "From the Oath According to Hippocrates insofar as a Christian May Swear It."

I raised my hand and took that Hippocratic Oath on a misty

June morning in 1949, as my father had just thirty years earlier on that identical spot of grass in the ineffably beautiful McGill quadrangle. The World Medical Association meeting at Geneva, in 1948, in the aftermath of the revelations of Nazi medical experiments, revised the oath marginally to include the pledge: "I will retain the utmost respect for Human Life from conception." Borrowing from the Declaration of Helsinki, the World Medical Association in 1964 restated the theme this way: "The health of my patient will be my first consideration."

Paradoxically, it was in that same year that Dr. Louis Lasagna, then a professor of medicine, pharmacology, and experimental therapeutics at Johns Hopkins University School of Medicine, sanitized the classic oath, eliminating the reference to abortion. Lasagna's version, the one usually used today, also purged the strictures against euthanasia (more of this later), sexual relations with patients, specific obligations to those who taught him (not just his professors, but the patients on whom he practiced as he learned the elements of medicine in medical school), and the crystalline sense of obligation to do good and avoid harming those in his charge.

As for retaining "the utmost respect for Human Life," here is what Lasagna's version has to say:

> Most especially must I tread with care in matters of life and death. If it is given to me to save a life, all thanks. But it may also be within my power to *take a life* [italics added]: this awesome responsibility must be faced with great humbleness and awareness of my own frailty. Above all, I must not play at God.

Let us then carry on for the late Dr. Lasagna, and update him as I'm sure he would approve. We have now a corporate version of the Hippocratic Oath, composed by David L. Schiedmayer at the Medical College of Wisconsin.

I swear by Humana and the American Hospital Supply Corporation and health maintenance organizations and preferred provider organizations and all the pre-payment systems and joint ventures, making them my witnesses, that I will fulfill according to my ability and judgment this oath and this covenant:

To hold the one who has taught me this business as equal to my corporation president and to live my life in partnership with him, and if he is in need of capital to give him some of mine, and to regard his offspring as equal to my colleagues and to teach them this business, for a fee....

I will neither give a deadly drug to anybody if asked for it, nor will I make a suggestion to that effect. Similarly, as an internist I will not perform an abortion. In fear of malpractice, I will guard my life and my business.

I will not use the knife unless I am a surgeon, but I will try to learn some form of endoscopy.

Into whatever clinics I may enter, I will come for the benefit of the injured, keeping myself far from all except capitated care for the underprivileged, especially if they are not covered by the group contract.

Things that I may see or hear in the course of treatment or even outside treatment regarding the life of human beings—things that one should never divulge outside—I will report to government commissions or administrators, or will use in my book.

If I fulfill this oath and do not violate it, may it be granted to me to enjoy life and business, and to be able to retire at the age of fifty in the sunbelt; if I transgress it and swear falsely, may Milwaukee be my lot.

Of all the oaths, incantations, pledges, declarations, and assorted other avowances, none in my opinion approaches the majesty and the touching humility of the Morning Prayer of the Physician composed by Rabbi Moses Maimon (Maimonides). Rambam, as he is known to Jewish scholars, was a skilled and conscientious physician—so skilled that he won appointment to the court of Saladin, the caliph of Cairo, as his personal physician. Rambam is more celebrated for his talmudic work, especially the second systematic codification of the Talmud, but his letter, "On the Management of Health," written to the son of the caliph at the turn of the thirteenth century, stands even today as a masterpiece of sound and temperate advice regarding one's duties and obligations to one's body. Here is a part of one of the many versions of the Morning Prayer:

Oh God, let my mind be ever clear and enlightened.

By the bedside of the patient let no alien thought deflect it.

Let everything that experience and scholarship have taught it be present in it and hinder it not in its tranquil work.

For great and noble are those scientific judgments that serve the purpose of preserving the health and lives of thy creatures.

Keep far from me the delusion that I can accomplish all things. Give me the strength, the will and the opportunity to amplify my knowledge more and more. Today I can disclose things in my knowledge which yesterday I would not have dreamed of, for the Art is great but the human mind presses on untiringly.

In the patient let me ever see only the man.

Thou, All-Bountiful One, hast chosen me to watch over the life and death of thy creatures. I prepare myself now for my calling. Stand Thou by me in this great task so that it may prosper, for without Thine aid man prospers not even in the smallest things.

I would not have been ashamed to have taken *that* oath on that misty June morning in 1949.

I recall with deep sadness that my father had been asked by the graduating class of the Cornell University Medical School—where he had taught obstetrics and gynecology for sixty years—to administer the oath to the members of the class on the stage of Carnegie Hall in the 1980s. It was the sanitized version, of course, but my father was then approaching ninety years of age and probably did not comprehend the difference. But I did. And I stood in the back of the auditorium and cringed a little for him, and the way in which they had—all unconsciously—debased him, for he was a strong believer in the tenets of the antique oath.

It has become fashionable in the circles of the *bien-pensants* bioethicists to denigrate the oath: to point with derision at its failures—for example, the omission of any reference to informed consent of the patient. Nevertheless, in a world as savage and as primitive as was the Island of Cos in the year 450 B.C., the expression of compassion, of respect for one's teachers, for life itself was and remains a monument to the beauty of the human soul and the dignity of the human person. Such monuments should not be hastily abandoned.

RUTH WAS A CAPTIVATING, INNOCENT, exceedingly intelligent young woman whom I met at a McGill dance in the autumn of 1945, in my first year in Montreal. She was seventeen and I was nineteen. We fell in love. She resembled the young Leslie Caron physically, and while I was no Gene Kelly or Mel Ferrer I actually enjoyed dancing with her (ordinarily I shun the dance floor). We began dating: movies, restaurants, ice skating, skiing, necking (is that word still in use?), and before long I was sleeping at her home on weekends. Her parents—Russian immigrants who had come to Canada in the thirties—and her brother had taken a liking to me, even in the face of an unforgettable gaffe: One evening, while all of us were sitting in her living room talking quietly, I reached into my wallet to extract a picture and the ubiquitous condom fell out. It did not simply drop to the floor but perversely it wheeled around the room and came to rest—like a roulette ball—directly beneath her father's feet. I mumbled something about a finger cot—a rubber device that fits over the examining finger of the obstetrician to allow him to examine rectally a woman in labor—and unceremoniously stuffed it back into my pocket. My explanation was undoubtedly less than convincing since I was only a first-year student at the time and had yet to see my first pregnant woman in a clinical setting.

Despite my unforgivable clumsiness, and despite our ski

weekends in the Laurentian mountains (her mother and father must have known we were sleeping together), the family and I remained close. In my third year I roomed with her brother and sister-in-law. We were spending more and more time together and talking seriously of marriage. And then she became pregnant.

When she missed her third period, I reluctantly stopped making esoteric diagnoses for her missed periods and called my father in New York; he instructed me to send her first morning urine specimen to him for testing in his hospital's laboratory. Two days later he called me and told me rather dolefully that the test was positive.

As I gaze backward over fifty years, I am struck by how naive I was. I had assumed that—as with all other matters of moment—my father would take care of everything. Quite the contrary: He wrote me a letter in which he enclosed five Canadian hundred-dollar bills, and in which he advised me to (a) find an abortionist in Catholic Montreal to do the abortion or (b) travel with Ruth to Plattsburg, to be married in the United States.

Thus was the first of my seventy-five thousand encounters with abortion. I had no inclination to marry; I was still facing another year and a half of medical school and five or six years of postgraduate (residency) training. My father had, for the first time in memory, failed me. I had secretly nursed a notion that he would arrange transportation for her to New York and carry out the abortion himself, concocting some reasonable indication for it. At the time I was unaware that the only loophole in the New York state law prohibiting abortion (dating from 1841) was a threat to the life of the woman.

I asked several of my classmates for the name of an abortionist, and eventually one did come through. I gave the name and telephone number to Ruth, and she arranged for it. The night before the abortion we slept together huddled in each other's arms; we both wept, for the baby we were about to lose, and for the love we both knew would be irreparably damaged by what we were about to do. It would never be the same for us.

The next day she took a taxi to the doctor's office. She insisted that I not accompany her, that I not be connected in any manner with the abortion for fear of jeopardizing my nascent medical career. I protested, but she was adamant that I not be anywhere near the scene of the crime. So we conspired to meet on the steps of the Redpath Library three hours later. I went to my classes that day but heard little of what was said. At the appointed time I sat down on the steps of the library. It was a soft late spring evening, and I heard the mournful sounds of a dystopic Portuguese *fado* being plucked out on a guitar across the quadrangle. I waited there four long hours, pacing, sobbing, bargaining with the Fates for her safety.

Finally, the taxi drew up to the steps. She was tremulous, ashen. I drew her out of the taxi. There was a spreading pool of blood on the floor of the cab. Reflexively, I paid the driver, then placed her tenderly on the steps of the library where she proceeded to weep copiously; the tears seemed to cascade from some inner inexhaustible reservoir, and her broken sobbing had the cadence and infinite sadness of some arcane prayer in an alien language. I cleaned her as best I could. Mercifully it was growing dark and the blood stains were blending into the evening gloom. I put her in the car I had borrowed, and drove her to her parents' house where I put her to bed with dispatch. I vowed to nurse her night and day until she was well. Miraculously, she recovered remarkably quickly and was able to attend her classes two days later.

She told me later that she had saved me $150 by bargaining the abortionist down; the abortionist was a frail, wizened old man who seemed forgetful and a little abstracted; midway through the procedure the bleeding had increased alarmingly and he seemed incapable of taking any definite action. So he told her to get off the table, get a taxi, and go home; she would pass the remainder of the pregnancy herself at home; if necessary, she might have to report to an emergency room at the local hospital in order to have the operation completed. Evidently, however, he had blundered into completing the operation himself, and nature took care of the rest.

I am some fifty years older now, but the experience is as fresh and quick in my mind as this morning's wedding, yesterday's funeral. Although for a brief period in the immediate aftermath we huddled together as co-conspirators in an unnameable crime, eventually we drifted apart. I am sure—despite her brave face, her loyalty and love, her pragmatic evaluation of the whole sorrowful gestalt—I am sure that in some melancholy corridor of her mind lurked the questions: Why didn't he marry me? Why couldn't we have had this baby? Why should I have had to imperil my life and my future children for the sake of his convenience and academic schedule? Will God punish me for what I have done by making me barren?

For myself, I was the consummate consequentialist; the questions crowding my mind dealt almost exclusively with her future health and reproductive ability: Had he damaged her to the point where she would no longer be able to conceive or bear children? What was to happen to our relationship? Would she sleep with me again, in the same loving, trusting, carefree way we had always had with each other? I did not concern myself with God and His incomprehensible vagaries (to *me*, at least, at that time and in that place). The stiff-backed Jewish atheist was already freezing into his mold.

As it turned out we saw each other but one more time after the school year ended; it was in a genteel shabby hotel in midtown New York in the searingly hot summer of 1948. We went to bed and had soundless, perfunctory sex. I dressed, went home, and mentally crossed the relationship off my list—resolving to pick up with someone else in my final year at McGill (I did). In 1954, on my way back from Pepperrell Air Force Base in St. John's, Newfoundland (I was then a captain in the air force), I purposefully delayed my return to New York to detour through Montreal; I was overwhelmingly curious as to what had happened to Ruth (this was six years after the abortion). At the airport I called her home, and was advised by her mother that she had married and had borne three lovely children. I wondered if she had ever told her husband about the abortion, and hoped she hadn't. And even at this remove—fifty-one years and counting—I am aware that I could have had grandchildren by now with this loving, beautiful woman.

Lessons? Too many and too sad to rehash here. Suffice it to say that it served as my introductory excursion into the satanic world of abortion. Nor was that the end of it for me *personally:* In the mid-sixties I impregnated a woman who loved me very much. She begged to keep the pregnancy, to have our child. I was just out of residency in obstetrics and gynecology, and was beginning to build a formidable practice in that specialty. I had already had two ruined marriages, both destroyed largely by my own selfish narcissism and inability to love. (I believe it was Father Zossima in *The Brothers Karamazov,* who defined hell as the suffering of one unable to love, and if this is true, I have served my sentence and then some.) I saw no practical way out of the situation, told her that I would not marry her and that I could not at that time afford to support a child (an egregious example of the coercion exercised by males in the abortion tragedy), and I not only demanded that she terminate the pregnancy as a condition of maintaining our relationship, but also coolly informed her that since I was one of the most skilled practitioners of the art, I myself would do the abortion. And I did.

What is it like to terminate the life of your own child? It was aseptic and clinical. She was put under anesthesia in the operating room of a major teaching hospital; I scrubbed my hands, gowned and gloved, chatted briefly with the scrub nurse, sat down on a little metal stool directly in front of the operating room table (after having examined her once again to verify the length of the pregnancy and the size of the uterus), and put the Auvard speculum in the vagina after prepping the area with antiseptic solution. I then grasped the cervix with two tenacula (hooks), infiltrated a solution of pitressin (a drug designed to firm up the uterine wall so I would be better able to appreciate the limits of the uterus and avoid perforating it), sounded the uterus (a sound is a long, thin steel instrument with centimeter markings on it, to show how far in the instruments can be safely placed), then dilated the cervix with the graduated shiny steel dilators. When the cervix was dilated to the desired diameter, I placed the hollow plastic cannula into the uterus and with a nod to the nurse indicated that I wished the suction to be turned on. When the gauge hit fifty-five millimeters of negative pressure I began sweeping the cannula around the interior of the uterus, watching the shards of tissue streaming through the hollow, translucent cannula on their way to the gauze trap where they would be collected, inspected, and then sent to the pathology laboratory for confirmation that pregnancy tissue had been—in our euphemistic vernacular—evacuated.

The procedure went on without incident, and I felt a fleeting gratification that I had done my usual briskly efficient job and left the operating room while she was still struggling up from general anesthesia. As an integral part of the procedure, every abortionist must examine the material in the gauze bag to assure that *all* the pregnancy tissue has been evacuated—to be certain none had been left behind to cause bleeding or infection later on. I peeled the bag open as was my custom, mentally gauged the amount of tissue and satisfied myself that it was proportionate to the length of the pregnancy; none had been left behind. I then took off my mask, stripped off my gloves and gown, picked up the hospital chart, and wrote the postoperative orders and the discharge note. I walked over to a dictating machine, dictated the operation onto a disk to be transcribed into an "op note" on the hospital chart, then made my way to the locker room to change my clothes while exchanging the usual badinage and cheery greetings with the other nurses and physicians and orderlies in the halls along the way to the lockers.

Yes, you may ask me: That was a concise terse report of what you *did,* but what did you feel? Did you not feel sad—not only because you had extinguished the life of an unborn child, but, more, because you had destroyed your *own* child? I swear to you that I had no feelings aside from the sense of accomplishment, the pride of expertise. On inspecting the contents of the bag I felt only the satisfaction of knowing that I had done a thorough job. You pursue me: You ask if perhaps for a fleeting moment or so I experienced a flicker of regret, a microgram of remorse? No and no. And that, dear reader, is the mentality of the abortionist: another job well done, another demonstration of the moral neutrality of advanced technology in the hands of the amoral.

Not to drag the European Holocaust yet one more time into the abortion conflict (I have steadfastly refused to draw the tempting parallel between the two in arguing the pro-life case; they are distinct and different phenomena), but what I felt in my starved, impoverished soul must have been closely akin to the swelling satisfaction of Adolf Eichmann, as he saw his tightly scheduled trains bearing Jews to the extermination camps leaving and arriving exactly on time, to keep the extermination machine moving with celebrated teutonic efficiency.

I have aborted the unborn children of my friends, colleagues, casual acquaintances, even teachers. There was never a shred of self-doubt, never a wavering of the supreme confidence that I was doing a major service to those who sought me out. My preoperative counseling consisted of a brief description of the procedure, pre- and postoperative instructions (no douching, no sexual relations, no tub baths for two weeks; start your oral contraceptive medication on the fifth day of your next period, which should begin about six weeks following this abortion; and see me again in my office for a check-up two weeks after the procedure), and a perfunctory assurance that the "procedure" (those of us who practiced it never spoke of it as an abortion, but rather used the term "termination of pregnancy" or "procedure") would have no effect on future fertility or on general health. We spoke with such confidence regarding these matters then, in the mid-sixties and the seventies; now it turns out there may be a relationship between abortion and breast cancer; thousands of women have indeed been rendered sterile in the aftermath of a botched abortion; and the death rate of women seeking abortion after the thirteenth week exceeds that of childbirth. The arrogance of those practicing medicine has always been recognized as an ugly appendage of the profession, but the massive hubris of the abortionist was and continues to be astonishing.

For every ten thousand Ruths there is one abortionist: icy; conscienceless; remorselessly perverting his medical skills; defiling his ethical charge; and helping, nay seducing, with his clinical calm, his oh-so-comforting professionalism, women into the act that comes closest to self-slaughter. It is no accident that the next step in the perverse mutation of medical skills is to be played where physicians are endowed by the state to assist, always in the name of compassion, in the act of suicide. How the world would have been changed had some misguided "expert" in the calculus of suffering climbed up on the cross and fed Jesus a dose of hemlock within an hour of His crucifixion.

CHAPTER 5

A Perfunctory Jew

IN MY INTERNSHIP YEAR AT Michael Reese Hospital in Chicago, a teaching hospital affiliated with Northwestern University, we were rotated monthly from one specialty area to another in an effort to give each of us a scientific overview of the profession. It was a Jewish hospital, the brand of medicine practiced was superb, and the academic teaching program for the interns and residents was exemplary. But the ethics of the institution—or lack of same—quickly became known to even the least morally percipient house officer. The amount of unnecessary surgery at that imposing institution was astonishing; the flourishing business of fee-splitting was scandalous. There was a sardonic joke among the members of the house staff that one had to knock loudly on the door of the men's room before entering, to give warning to the attending physicians divvying up kickbacks from patients.

I do not believe that this ethical vacuum was a result of the hospital's Jewishness—I know my profession too well for that. Rather, the moral tenor of the place was lowered, as in the case of many Jewish institutions today, as in the house in which I was raised, by its lack of Judaism. This Jewish hospital, supported by funds from Jewish organizations and individual donors, had not one single space devoted to prayer, meditation, ceremony, or observation of the most holy days of the Jewish calendar. Even in an Episcopal institution like St. Luke's Hospital in New York City in which I worked for many years, the front entrance of the hospital framed a regal sweep of marble stairs leading to a simple hushed chapel open night and day for patients, relatives, even staff members and other employees. On solemn Christian holidays there were always services several times daily. At the Catholic hospital at which I have worked, similar religious facilities were available, and their use was encouraged by the administration of the hospital. Why was it that the Jewish hospital had no such space, encouraged no activity of the soul?

No faith. But always there was in its place the *yiddishkeit,* albeit at Michael Reese Hospital a spleeny variety: Jewish jokes would fly around the operating and delivery rooms, and the members of the attending and house staff would bawl Yiddish terms at each other with evident delight (they were either European immigrants themselves who had fled the Nazi scourge or the sons and daughters of immigrants), even to the extent of incorporating Yiddishisms into their orders to the nurses (who were almost entirely non-Jewish, drawn from southern Illinois and neighboring Indiana) and into their progress notes in the medical records. In short, that hospital was another comforting fuzzy Jewish cocoon for me, as if the west side of Manhattan had been extended to Chicago. Even the nurses slung the lingo around with the breezy assurance of *yeshivabuchers.* I clearly recall being told by a black nurse in the delivery suite (my first rotation in my first month at Michael

Reese) that one of the orders I had written was *ganz meshugeneh,* i.e., really crazy. One is, after all, always at home in one's past.

MY FIRST WIFE WAS JEWISH, a college graduate, and as emotionally jejune as I. Her father was a man of not inconsiderable means (her mother had died when she was thirteen, and she had never warmed to her stepmother). Her younger brother was fond of his sister in his awkward adolescent way (he was in his late teens when she and I met). We decided to marry after only two months of dating.

She was a year older than I, had graduated the liberal arts program of a well-respected university in New York City, and had become enmeshed in an uncomfortable relationship with the married lawyer for whom she worked. A blind date had been arranged for us by an intern in my group at New York Hospital. (It was my second internship, after Michael Reese.) We liked each other immediately; she was as Jewish as I, i.e., her household had the identical *yiddishkeit* that mine did, and she was as casual and as perfunctory a Jew as I.

My father and her father had taken a liking to each other from their first meeting. They had sprung from the same Eastern European and germanic stock, and although her father had been born in Europe, his family had migrated to the United States when he was just a child. He spoke Yiddish fluently, observed the Jewish holidays with the same feigned devotion as my father, and had suffered the same degree of grinding poverty in his childhood. In short, if the marriage had been an arranged one, it could not have paired two more theoretically matched people.

The wedding took place in the study of Rabbi Louis Newman, the leader of the Congregation Rodeph Sholem, on a
stifling August afternoon. The synagogue was on the upper west
side of Manhattan. It was an imposing building, one that I had
never entered before, although my mother and father had bought
tickets for seats during the high holy days at that temple.

Rabbi Newman was a beefy, diffident, fiftyish man who had
achieved a modest reputation for Jewish scholarship and was
considered a model of aristotelian rationalism—a man of the
golden mean, not *meshugeneh* Orthodox (my father's words).
His study reflected an air of impressive scholasticism: deeply sat-
isfying leather furniture, muted lamps, imposing banks of
books, and an unusually spacious desk reminiscent of a runway
for a jumbo jet.

I recall that on the morning preceding the ceremony, while
showering at her apartment, I had serious second thoughts. I
did not truly love this woman, although I liked and respected
her. I was not intensely attracted sexually, although we were
reasonably compatible in that way. We came from different sub-
cultures of the Jewish community, she from Brooklyn and I
from Manhattan. I was at home in the world of books and
ideas, she had very little interest in these matters. On the other
hand, I was tired of living in hot, stuffy, airless hospital rooms;
weary of trying to live on the absurdly low stipend we were
then paid as house officers in the hospital ($37.50 monthly, with
food, room, and laundry thrown in); and bored with living tran-
siently with a seemingly endless string of female companions.
She had an attractive, spacious, air-conditioned apartment on
the upper east side of Manhattan and enough money to afford
us a car, and she was a comely woman of respectable back-
ground and educational advantage.

I subjected myself to a veritable voir dire in the shower and concluded that I might as well go ahead with the ceremony, and if things didn't work out I could always get a divorce. There was no feeling of deep commitment, certainly not of sacrament; not the slightest trace of awe of the moment or the nature of the act. Truly, I was a child of the movies: By the late forties and early fifties, marriage was for Hollywood a delightful lark, a light and frothy experience that marked the end of an exuberant, often topsy-turvy, love affair. Most important, my father had given his grudging approval to the merger despite his own venomous hatred of all things linking men to women in other than a purely sexual, and noncontractual, manner.

Rabbi Newman maintained his air of epistemic solemnity; muttered a series of Hebrew prayers with what seemed to me to be calcified, mechanical translations for the intellectually unwashed; then gradually began to swell up to at least twice his size as he came to the part of the ceremony wherein he grandly pronounced us husband and wife. We kissed dutifully, I smashed the drinking glass (prudently wrapped in a thick napkin) that commemorates the fall of Jerusalem in 70 A.D., and it was done.

The wedding party of twenty repaired to the Starlight Roof of the Waldorf Astoria Hotel for dinner and dancing. As I study the photograph taken that night in that place, I am struck by the absence of joy in the faces of those who attended, the melancholy lurking behind the pasted-on smiles, as if all had just witnessed a not-especially-satisfying auto-da-fé. God, I suppose, was the missing guest.

My premarital escape plan was self-fulfilling. In 1953, I interrupted my final residency in obstetrics and gynecology at Woman's Hospital in New York to enlist in the Air Force. I was sent to do obstetrics and gynecology in St. John, Newfoundland—with diverting little excursions to Greenland, Iceland, and Labrador. My wife and I had a largely unspoken agreement that we would not attempt to conceive a child (she joined me in Newfoundland a month after I arrived there), and the marriage was soon reduced to polite interchanges and perfunctory sex. By mutual agreement and with exquisite politesse, we decided to part after I was discharged from the service. I moved back into the hospital while she continued to occupy a small apartment in Yonkers. Once the appropriate documents had been prepared, I flew down to Mexico (divorce laws were still rigorous in New York state), held up my hand in the company of perhaps fifteen other Americans, mumbled "yes" in response to an interminable civil procedure conducted in Spanish, and signed a singularly large register in the space marked with an *X;* the marriage was kaput. The division was as bloodless, ritualistic, and meaningless as the merger.

The marriage had lasted exactly four and a half years. We parted civilly. She later moved to San Francisco, and I never heard from her again.

I think now that the marriage failed precisely *because* she was Jewish in the same mode as I: uncommitted, spiritually irresolute, materially obsessed, and wise to the beguiling ways of another modern Jew. She had, after all, been brought up in an almost identical mise-en-scène as I, and had been taught to discount the charming little mannerisms, the misdirectional emotional tricks, and the alluring cynicism of the modern secular Jewish male. To be blunt, she was wise to me and my practiced artifices, and we quickly became bored with each other. Divorce was inevitable, and when the subject arose, it was to no one's surprise—or dismay.

As I MENTIONED, my residency years in obstetrics and gynecology were at the then world-renowned Woman's Hospital, alas no longer with us. The hospital was founded in 1855 by a southern physician, J. Marion Sims, and was the first specialty hospital devoted entirely to the treatment of disorders of women in the United States. When I arrived there in 1952, I had already put in several years of postgraduate training in the areas of general surgery and urology at large university teaching hospitals, Michael Reese and New York Hospital, the teaching center for Cornell University Medical School. When I had my first glimpse of Woman's Hospital in its most recent incarnation (it had been reconstructed in the Harlem section of Manhattan in 1900), I was a little aghast. This hulking baroque monstrosity with its copper mansard roof, its courtly porte cochere, and its stained glass windows, resembled more the laboratory of Dr. Frankenstein than a modern high-tech medical center. Nevertheless, the staff of teaching and practicing physicians and surgeons was superb; the clinics, which were the backbone of any great medical teaching institution, were enormous since the hospital was located in a poverty-stricken area; and the esprit of the nursing staff was extraordinary. Many of the nurses had been there twenty or more years, and they contributed significantly to the teaching of young physicians in training. My father had been on the staff of that hospital for twenty-five years when I arrived, and was in a position of considerable seniority; he was acknowledged to be one of the teaching luminaries of the institution, owing largely to his vast experience teaching medical students at Cornell Medical School, where he spent the other 50 percent of his professional time.

There was only one jarring note in this otherwise edenic learning experience: Much of the physician and residency staff was openly anti-Semitic. My father was one of only two Jews on the staff, and I was to be the first Jewish resident in the one-hundred-year history of this institution. I was informed, on my first day of duty at Woman's Hospital, that the chief resident in obstetrics had passed the word that he would not work with a Jew and that I should probably look for a residency elsewhere. My informant was a senior resident, an Italian Catholic who had experienced a similar bias when he had first started his residency.

I had encountered a less malignant and less frontal bigotry at New York Hospital, where I was only the second Jew in the surgical residency program, but my rather pallid brand of Jewry combined with my devotion to duty had made the issue more or less moot by the time I completed my program there. At Woman's Hospital, the air was fetid with intolerance and I was sorely tempted to quit the program after the first week. My father counseled me to be patient, do my work, and eschew any confrontations with the anti-Semitic clique. Meanwhile, he was busy rounding up a coalition of the more liberal members of the attending staff and residents. He then confronted the chief resident and the chief surgeon of the hospital and warned them that if there were any unpleasant incidents traceable to anti-Semitic behavior, he would immediately inform the Anti-Defamation League of the B'Nai Brith, as well as newspapers, television reporters, and assorted other opinion makers. My father was short but blustery and when aroused would waggle an index finger under the nose of his opponent while bellowing his version of the argument. I do not delude myself into believing that he converted the bigots into the disciples of Gandhi, but the bigotry had the decency to veil itself thereafter and I was permitted to do my work in a reasonably neutral climate of tolerance. Moreover, the chief resident finished his program six months after I arrived, and the pressure I had felt disappeared with his departure.

Parenthetically, I am amused (and pleased immeasurably) to see that the residency program at St. Luke's-Roosevelt Hospital Center (which devoured Woman's Hospital over the succeeding twenty years) now has an Asian as its chairman and professor; the attending physician staff is at least one-half Jewish, two-thirds female, and at least one-third black or Hispanic. The same proportions apply to the resident staff.

I had encountered anti-Semitism before. But in my youthful naiveté I had thought that those who practiced medicine would be civilized, or at least too subtle, to allow themselves the intellectually humiliating brew of bigotry.

I recall that when I was fifteen years old my father and mother had planned to spend my father's first vacation after twenty-three years of practice in New England, touring college campuses in that part of the country. When we drove into Wolfboro, New Hampshire, and registered at the local hotel—with an eye to exploring Dartmouth University the next day—my father was asked by the desk clerk if the name "Nathanson" was a Scandinavian one. He retorted that it was about as Scandinavian as spaghetti, it was Jewish and what business was it of the clerk's anyway. The clerk backed out of the registration area to be replaced by the manager of the hotel, who politely but firmly informed my father that the hotel was "restricted," a repellent euphemism for no Jews allowed. To my astonishment and chagrin, my father turned around, motioned us to follow him, and we slunk out of that hotel wordlessly. In the car, proceeding toward more hospitable lodgings farther south toward Boston, my father whipped himself up to a fine lather vowing to report the man, promising to write a letter to the editor of the *New York Times,* and resolving to lodge a complaint with the B'Nai Brith Anti-Defamation League. Whether he carried out any or all of these threats to this day I still do not know, but I was left with the virtually ineradicable impression that outside of New York City and its large community of wealthy and influential Jews, we were aliens in our own land.

Anti-Semitism *was* rampant when I was a child, but not in my childhood. The incident in New Hampshire had taken place in the late thirties, an especially distressing era for American Jews. Father Charles Coughlin was disseminating his singularly venomous anti-Semitic gospel via a weekly address from his parish in Detroit to forty-five radio stations across the country, and it was estimated that at least four million Americans tuned in to him regularly. By one estimate probably fifteen million people had listened to Coughlin at least once; his office was receiving approximately eighty thousand letters a week (virtually all favorable), and he maintained a staff of 105 employees to read and respond to the letters. His newsletter, *Social Justice,* had a comparably wide audience and was pervaded by an anti-Semitism so fulsome that it would put Julius Streicher's Nazi publication *Volkische Beobachter* to shame.

In those days Colonel Charles Lindbergh, perhaps the most admired citizen in the United States and certainly the most popular, accepted a medal from Adolf Hitler. In 1941 in a speech in Des Moines, Lindbergh castigated the Jews, accusing them of pushing America into World War II with the active connivance of the Roosevelt administration. Lindbergh went on to claim: "Their greatest danger to this country lies in their large ownership and influence in our motion pictures, our press, our radio, and our government." Sound familiar? The

African American anti-Semitic lunatic fringe (Farrakhan, Muhammed, Jeffries, and company) have ripped off Lindbergh to a fare-thee-well and are successfully peddling this arrant poison to a disaffected underclass anxious only to find a scapegoat for their economic and political misfortunes. The scapegoat is, as all through history, the Jew.

For the most part I was effectively shielded from this whiny garbage. I would hear my father pace the living room and condemn Coughlin in loud and excoriating terms; my mother would shake her head sadly at the mention of Lindbergh's name. But I was insulated in the Jewish quarter (*not* ghetto; we were not prisoners), being educated in the predominantly Jewish school, and in the summer I was sent to camps owned and administered by Jews, with, again, a predominantly Jewish population. Hence, the episode in that joyless little hotel in New Hampshire was something of a cultural shock, although later, with increasing exposure to the outside *goyische* world, I became increasingly aware of the endemic nature of anti-Semitism and increasingly contemptuous of those who openly practiced it. In an otherwise civilized society, arrogance has its uses: In America one can deal with anti-Semitism by clicking off the great scholars, musicians, scientists, financiers, and other towering figures in the Jewish-American community.

As A YOUNG MAN, a young doctor, my sense of Jewishness—this can surely come as no revelation to any student of social and religious America—was fundamentally communitarian. We ignored ourselves as Hebrews while reveling in the spirit of *yiddishkeit:* its traditions, its dialect, its inside jokes, and its inchoate sense of intellectual superiority. Always there was that sense of huddling together as Jews. With deep shame, I recall an episode in the mid-fifties that illustrates perfectly that dismaying *zeitgeist*.

During my days in premedical education at Cornell University, I had made the acquaintance of one Mark Lazansky, a Jewish premedical student from Brooklyn. Although never close at Cornell, we met again at Michael Reese Hospital as interns, and it was at this point that we became fast friends. Mark had been casually interested in left-wing causes at Cornell (the Second World War was then reaching its zenith, and the USSR was our putative ally) and had attended a few meetings of the far Left groups—but had never to my knowledge joined any of them or even expressed an interest in doing so. Incidentally, most of these groups were organized and led by Jewish students.

After our intern year was finished at Michael Reese, Mark and I remained in close touch (we shared also a consuming interest in the works of the great American humorist S. J. Perelman and would quote great swatches of his best work to each other at the slightest provocation). Together, we went to Washington in the early part of 1953 to enlist in the Air Force in the hope that we would be stationed together in some facility in or around New York City. *My* commission papers came through in short order, and I was assigned for basic training at Gunter Air Force Base in Alabama. Mark's application for commission was obstructed. I was later informed that he was never granted a commission but was received into the Air Force as an enlisted man although he was by this time an accomplished orthopedic surgeon—a specialty the Air Force required far more urgently than an obstetrician-gynecologist. We lost touch with each other, but I subsequently learned that he had been assigned to a base in Arkansas and was, as an enlisted man, performing most of the complicated orthopedic surgery at that base. He had been denied his commission because of anonymously reported left-wing associations and advocacy of communist causes at Cornell; I *knew* that nothing could be further from the truth.

In an effort to clear his name while in the service, Mark engaged a prestigious law firm in New York City. This was the McCarthy era, and Senator Joe McCarthy had now joined battle with the U.S. Army in the notorious Army-McCarthy hearings. Mark then wrote me a letter and asked that I appear as a character witness for him in an appearance before a McCarthy subcommittee (I was by this time a captain in the U.S. Air Force, and chief of the obstetrical and gynecological service in my area of the command). My first impulse was to rush to his defense, but on second thought I decided to consult the chief counsel on the base, Herbert Cohen. Cohen and I had become friends after I had delivered his wife of their child, and I had no hesitancy in seeking his advice on this matter. Cohen and I discussed it; it was Cohen's opinion as a lawyer that if I appeared I would automatically become suspect myself, that I could lose my own commission, and that Jews in the armed forces should generally keep a low profile and certainly *not* antagonize anyone as powerful (and undoubtedly anti-Semitic) as Senator Joseph McCarthy.

I mulled over Herb Cohen's advice, solicited the opinions of several other of my Jewish friends on the physician staff—all of whom agreed with Cohen—and then (I cringe with shame as I write these words some forty years later) wrote Mark's lawyers that I was far too busy to become involved in this mini-Dreyfuss matter, and they would have to find someone else. I never heard from Mark again.

Well, you might say, the *shtetl* mentality would require that you spring to the defense of your fellow Jew, that you leave the pack to pick up the wounded and helpless. I'm afraid not: the dictates of self-preservation, moral cowardice, the ancient tradition of huddling together in the cellars of czarist Russia while the Cossacks whirled about with their snapping whips and whispering swords, the ultra-cautious effacement of the foreign Jew in a strange land (we are always foreigners, wherever we are) all conspired to lead me to an act of monumental cowardice. I not only lost a valued friend, I crystallized my self-image as the foreigner, the intimidated stranger, the rootless, causeless cowering Jew. It is probably no sheer coincidence that my marriage commenced to break up at this point, that I began to seek the company of non-Jews, and that I soon would break with my father. Nor was it pure chance that I found myself soon thereafter married to a non-Jew and in company with a man who veiled his Jewishness so cleverly that for years I never was sure whether Larry Lader was Jewish or not (he was, and is).

CHAPTER 6

Poor and Pregnant

DURING THOSE YEARS IN WOMAN'S HOSPITAL, I began to believe my father was not the infallible godhead I had conceived him to be. As a resident I worked with him frequently on cases or in surgery. Then as his son, I joined his practice, or rather I moved into his office. Not only did he not ask me to be his partner, I remember the arrangement being more like a particularly degrading and impoverishing form of sharecropping. His tyranny, however, I was used to. What shocked me was his vulnerability. When I was assigned to assist him with surgery or with a particularly difficult obstetrical matter, I perceived that he lacked confidence in himself: He would *constantly* ask if what he was doing was safe or prudent or harmless. During major pelvic surgery the need to constantly reassure the operating surgeon was not only a distraction, but was time-wasting and even a little demoralizing. If the private attending surgeon was unsure of himself, think how the resident-in-training would feel.

It was also during this time that I began to cultivate feelings of remorse for my relationship with my mother, and consequently I communicated with her and visited with her more often than I had in the past. This action infuriated my father, to the extent that by the time I had finished my first year of practice he asked me to leave his office. We stopped speaking.

But the real break came with my second marriage. Rosemary was not Jewish, and he resumed speaking to me long enough to tell me that if I went through with the marriage I would be utterly cut off from him. I married, and not only did he not speak to me again for the succeeding ten years, but he also became my most implacable enemy. When I was proposed for membership in the New York Obstetrical Society (a prestigious sodality of outstanding members of the obstetrical community) some years later, he persuaded several of his cronies in that society (of which he had been a member for many years) to blackball me and exclude me from membership. My god had failed me, and those were black days indeed.

I finished my OB-GYN training in February of 1957. I packed up my things and moved out of the hospital into a cramped, shabby room in a seedy hotel nearby. This was before I remarried. I was in a state of equal parts of puzzlement, dismay, melancholia, and futility as I pondered my rather bleak prospects: My father and I were not speaking to each other; I was heavily in debt from my divorce from my first wife, Carol; and I was lonely and suffering from a terminal case of "hospitalitis." (After living in hospitals for so many years, one becomes dependent on the services the hospital provides, the schedules by which one wakes, works, eats, and sleeps.) At the conclusion of the first week of living in that gloomy, depressing hotel room, I was suddenly informed that the chief resident in obstetrics had committed suicide, and since the hospital had no one immediately available to replace him, the administrator asked me if I would move back into the hospital and the residency program, to finish out his six-month term of service. I did not need to be asked twice, and moved forthwith.

IT WAS AT WOMAN'S HOSPITAL that I had my first real lessons in caring for the health of the poor. Although the staff of private physicians would admit their well-to-do patients to that hospital and we residents would assist the private doctors in the operating and delivery rooms, the clinics to which the poor repaired were run largely by the resident staff. The poorest of the poor comprised our patient population. Although we treated these women with a reasonable degree of respect (for the times), there was a good deal of patriarchal condescension in our professional relations with these poor women: We would call them by their first names, we regarded them primarily as teaching material ("Hey, Joe, come on into my examining room and look at this great prolapse; I've got her booked for a vaginal hysterectomy next week"). Inquiries or questioning of a physician's instructions by the patient (mainly black or Hispanic) was regarded as rebellion. I can recall instances in which the patient's questioning of the resident's decision—especially regarding the need for surgery—would be met with a not-so-polite invitation to find another clinic in another hospital.

In my first months of residency, I was struck by the enormous disparity in the rate of spontaneous miscarriage between the private patients of the staff physicians (minimal), and the poor patients in our clinic population (high). At first I put it down to economic factors: poor nutrition, late (or no) prenatal care, and grand multiparity (having had five or more babies before). But the more I pondered this matter the less satisfied I became with the answers I had concocted. Finally, a kindly senior resident took me aside and explained the medical facts of life: At least two-thirds of the clinic females ambulanced to our emergency room in the middle of the night, bleeding profusely and in severe pain, were the victims of botched illegal abortions, *not* spontaneous miscarriages. Someone—physician, nurse midwife, grandma—had started the abortion with one of a variety of objects ranging from a standard curette to a knitting needle, then forwarded the patient to the nearest emergency room for treatment. That same senior resident gave me the magic formula for identifying the illegal abortion: two small, almost indiscernible marks on the anterior (front) lip of the cervix (neck of the womb); those were the marks of the tenaculum, an instrument that clamps onto the cervix to steady it while another instrument is thrust through the closed cervix into the uterus to disrupt the ongoing implanted pregnancy. Armed with that knowledge I began to look for the tenaculum marks in those poor unfortunates. Of course the resident was correct: at least two-thirds of them *were* the victims of illegal induced abortion.

The rest of the story has a curiously anachronistic cast to it— we are now in the twenty-third year of legal abortion in the United States, and there are at least two generations of women who have grown up with legal abortion as a given, an entitlement if not a right. Those of us practicing gynecology no longer see the results of illegal induced abortion: the raging fevers; the torn and obstructed intestines; the shredded uteri requiring immediate hysterectomy; the raging infections leaving many women sterile, exhausted, in chronic pain, terrified of another pregnancy if they remained fertile. In the forties and fifties—before the advent of better-trained gynecologists, powerful antibiotics, efficient contraception, improved blood transfusion technology, and the development of the concept of intensive care—our gynecology wards were filled with these broken, maimed bodies.

We gynecologists did what we could—for our middle-class, well-off, unwillingly pregnant patients. I referred many of my patients for abortion in Puerto Rico, at the offices of a Dr. "Juan Rodriguez" (not his real name). Rodriguez had trained at a major gynecologic hospital in the United States, then had returned to his native Puerto Rico to start a practice and—with the cooperation of the local authorities, abortion being illegal in Puerto Rico—to do a few abortions on the side. Word-of-mouth did its work, and his abortion practice soon flourished. Ninety percent of his abortion patients came from the eastern seaboard of the United States, and he very soon amassed a fortune. This was counterproductive for those of us referring our pregnant patients to him: As he grew wealthier, he would take longer and more expensive vacations in Europe and we would be at a loss. Nevertheless, he continued to function as our court of last resort until the laws changed in the United States. Then, ironically, with a crackdown by the authorities in Puerto Rico who evidently were receiving insufficient *baksheesh*, I began to receive pregnant women sent by *him* from Puerto Rico for abortion in New York.

The Rodriguez caper, unstable in its very nature, functioned satisfactorily enough for our more affluent women, although I personally received a rather rude awakening one day in 1964 while changing planes in San Juan. I had a few hours to kill, and rather than sit around idly in the airport I decided to take a taxi and visit Dr. Rodriguez. I had spoken with him innumerable times on the phone about patient problems but we had never met. I arrived at his office, a blockhouse of gray stucco, strode confidently in, and introduced myself to him—he had no receptionist, nurse, or other ancillary help at the time. I was taken a little aback by the modest dimensions of his facility, considering the enormous number of patients he was receiving on a steady basis from the Boston–New York–Washington corridor. But his fluent English, his confident demeanor, and the banks of impressive diplomas behind his desk did serve to assuage my anxieties—until I saw his "operating room." It had cream-colored walls, two large windows open to the street (a steady stream of friends and acquaintances poked their heads through the windows and proffered their greetings to both of us), and an antique examining table that looked as if it had been designed by Andreas Vesalius, the noted sixteenth-century Paduan anatomist. He proudly displayed the table to me and offered that it was so designed to allow him to inject sodium pentothal (an anesthetic) into the patient at the head of the table, then rapidly to place the patient in stirrups, dilate the cervix and scrape out the uterus in a flash, then scoot back to the head of the table to wake the patient up. In short, he was anesthesiologist, nurse, and physician simultaneously. He must have noted my anxiety following his exegesis on his technique; he once more ushered me into his consultation room and gave me a guided tour through his various diplomas, licenses, accreditations, societal affiliations, and the like. This did not calm my nerves, since on close examination I noted that the paper products so flamboyantly displayed on his wall amounted to *nothing* medically: every credential, society, and license he had was purchasable. But he was the only game in town; I pulled myself together, mentally shrugged, shook his hand, politely declined an offer of a modest kickback for every patient I referred, and was on my way back to the airport—wiser but shakier than before.

Although I continued to refer patients to Rodriguez (and to those—even less distinguished?—physicians who filled in for him during his frequent vacations), a few cracks began to appear in what had heretofore appeared to be a monolithic opposition to abortion on demand. In the mid-1960s, the model American Law Institute (ALI) statute on abortion was published, and provided for abortion in the case of pregnancy by incest, rape, fetal deformity (unspecified as to how serious), or medical conditions accompanying the pregnancy that reasonable physicians would certify would threaten the woman's life *or health*. By 1967, the state of Colorado had adopted this law—with the restriction that only bona fide residents of the state were qualified under the law. North Carolina soon followed in adopting the ALI model, and California. The residency requirements had no practical force. Still, these laws served almost exclusively the middle class and slighted the poor pregnant women in other states who could not afford the hegira to states with liberalized laws, let alone Japan, where abortion had been legal since 1948 and was being carried out on a mass scale. In 1968, Great Britain weighed in with a permissive abortion statute. I began referring pregnant women there since there was virtually no limit to the gestational age at which the British physicians would terminate a pregnancy. I myself paid a visit to London twenty years ago and watched an acquaintance—one Dr. David Sopher—dispose of thirty-two pregnancies (all over eighteen weeks) between nine in the morning and two in the afternoon. At approximately noon he had the nurse push up his mask and feed him a glass of orange juice through a straw, all the time chatting amiably about where the best shirt-makers were to be found in London, and mounting a learned discussion of the virtues of the Rolls Royce vs. the Bentley and the Mercedes Benz. I was duly impressed and had absolutely no hesitancy in referring pregnant women to him—if they could afford the trip.

That was the rub: what to do about those poverty-stricken women still being ambulanced into our emergency rooms bleeding profusely, in septic shock, in cardiac failure, or even dead on arrival. These were the women who needed our attention: Illegal abortion was in 1967 the number one killer of pregnant women.

And then I met Larry Lader.

CHAPTER 7

The Statesman

WILLIAM OBER WAS, BY TRAINING AND PRACTICE, a fine, highly skilled pathologist. His avocation was history, in particular the history of medicine. I have before me a book he wrote in 1979 entitled *Boswell's Clap: Medical Analyses of Literary Men's Afflictions.* It is an elegant, witty, and meticulously researched work on the physical and mental ills of such luminaries as Boswell, Swinburne, Keats, Cowper, Collins, Shadwell, and Smart. He explores the question of whether Socrates actually died of a dose of hemlock (he concludes that he did), and excavates into the lives of other physician-writers such as Chekhov and William Carlos Williams (both come off rather well). The section on Boswell reveals that eminent Scot suffered nineteen separate attacks of gonorrhea during his incorrigible trafficking with prostitutes. One marvels at the energy of the man, to have written one of the great biographies of all time while simultaneously whoring and gambling at a pace that would exhaust a man half his age and twice his size.

When I received an invitation to a dinner party at Ober's house in 1967 (he had learned that we shared an interest in Joyce), I immediately accepted, expecting an unusually stimulating evening. I could not know that it would change my life, thrust me into the vortex of the most contentious issue of our times, and ultimately lead me into re-examining my soul.

At dinner I was seated next to a cadaverous-appearing man with a rasping voice. He introduced himself as Lawrence Lader. We made the usual small talk and, as I was about to turn away to converse with the party on my other side (I cannot for the life of me remember who *that* was), he casually mentioned that he had just published a book on abortion, a book in which he had analyzed the prevailing laws restricting abortion in the United States, torn apart all the arguments for retaining those laws, and demanded that all such laws be struck down as medically unsound and legally unconstitutional. What he was advocating was nothing less than free access to abortion for all unwillingly pregnant women, the procedure to be priced so low as to be within the means of the poorest.

If there was one thing I was more interested in talking about than Joyce, it was abortion. We began to talk, and the conversation lasted eight years; in that span of time, every abortion law in the United States was struck down, the lines between pro- and anti-abortionists were drawn, and the battle joined. The casualty list of that war at this writing is so long that it would take six hundred Vietnam Memorial walls to list all who have perished.

Lader was a fascinating farrago of paradox. He was economically secure, having been left a considerable trust fund upon the death of his father many years before. Yet, he had worked for Vito Marcantonio, the only card-carrying communist ever to be elected to the U.S. House of Representatives. He was an ardent feminist and a great admirer of Margaret Sanger, and a patriarchal bully in his own household. He and his wife Joan, a cheery Scot who had all but given up a promising career in grand opera for him, lived in a splendid apartment on lower Fifth Avenue in Greenwich Village; but the furnishings of the place were startlingly ascetic and of a shabby gentility. He was Jewish, but in all the years I knew him he never discussed his Jewishness. He was an erudite man of exceedingly refined tastes but was maddeningly pedantic and precious in his dealings with friends and allies. And he was obsessed with abortion.

Partly because we lived near each other, Larry and I soon were spending a great deal of time in each other's company. He was a magazine writer with no fixed hours of work, so he would accommodate graciously my very busy schedule of practicing gynecology; teaching at Cornell Medical School; reading, writing about, and teaching Joyce; all the while trying to balance domestic life against these various duties and pursuits. Our subject was invariably abortion, if not directly then indirectly: With the election of the allegedly conservative Richard Nixon in 1968, we counted ourselves set back temporarily, but certainly not discouraged or defeated. When Martin Luther King and Robert Kennedy were assassinated in the same year, we discussed these monumental events primarily as whether they were good or bad for the abortion revolution that we were by this time scheming. Even Denny McLain's heroic thirty-game-winning season (a feat no major league pitcher had brought off in thirty-five years) had to be analyzed through the abortion prism. (On balance, McLain's feat was bad as it distracted the public from serious issues such as the sexual revolution.)

In short I found, to my surprise, that I had been subtly dragooned into planning political strategy with Lader. By 1969, we were setting the agenda for a meeting of the leading national pro-abortion figures to take place in Chicago. Out of that meeting would emerge the fledgling National Association for Repeal of Abortion Laws (NARAL), later changed to the National Abortion Rights Action League, and currently styling itself as the National Abortion and Reproductive Rights Action League. We were putting out feelers to Betty Friedan and her corps of feminists to join us in the revolution, coalition building with the Woodstock nation, and crushing the dinosaurs in the movement who would settle for watered-down measures such as the model ALI law. Lader, I, and a handful of others such as Howard Moody, then pastor of the Judson Memorial Church in Manhattan's Greenwich Village, were the radicals, the bolsheviks. We would settle for nothing less than striking down all existing abortion statutes and substituting abortion on demand.

Our first target of opportunity was the New York state statute prohibiting abortion unless the pregnancy threatened the life of the pregnant woman. The manipulation of the media was crucial, but easy with clever public relations, especially a steady drumfire of press releases disclosing the dubious results of surveys and polls that were in effect self-fulfilling prophecies, proclaiming that the American people already did believe what they soon would believe: that all reasonable folk knew that abortion laws had to be liberalized. In the late sixties and early seventies, the media trenches were peopled with young, cynical, politically case-hardened, well-educated radicals who were only too anxious to upset the status quo, roil the waters, and rattle the cages of authority.

Of course, the time was ripe. Something mysterious but momentous had happened with the historical confluence of the assassination of John F. Kennedy, the torturous slow descent into the Vietnam quagmire, and the coming to political age of the baby boomer generation—perhaps the most spoiled, pampered, and politically ignorant (though well-educated) generation in this nation's history. These elements simmered into a brew as combustible as nitroglycerine and as unstable as a quark. A tsunami of antiauthoritarianism washed across the land, carrying with it the drug culture, the sexual revolution, the pernicious infiltration of pornography, violent crime, and the contemptuous denigration of religion. Certainties as unquestioned as the U.S. Constitution itself trembled.

Lader sniffed the winds of change. He knew, standing in the wreckage of the sixties and watching the pillars of certainty cracking and crumbling around him, that his time had come around, that it was the perfect historical moment in which to strike against senescent rheumy-eyed Authority.

He also sensed that Authority had to have a familiar form, a discernible shape, a clear and preferably noxious identity, and if at all possible a shamefully malevolent past to point to. What better than the Roman Catholic Church? It was spawned in blood; it had exiled, tortured, broken, and murdered millions of heretics and their followers. The church was then actively supporting the Vietnam War, opposing the sexual revolution, denouncing the drug culture, and dragging its feet on the Civil Rights Movement. No more perfect straw man could ever have been devised.

And so we set to work, and it was like shooting fish in a barrel. Though at the start the Flat Earth Society would have seemed to constitute a greater threat to the Roman Catholic Church in 1969 than NARAL did, we attacked at every opportunity. Our favorite tack was to blame the church for the death of every woman from a botched abortion. There were perhaps three hundred or so deaths from criminal abortions annually in the United States in the sixties, but NARAL in its press releases claimed to have data that supported a figure of five thousand. Fortunately, the respected biostatistician Dr. Christopher Tietze was our ally. Though he never actually staked himself to a specific number, he never denied the authenticity of these claims.

Lader's New York state campaign was a paradigm of political gamesmanship and social warfare. He proceeded on Machiavelli's maxim: "There is nothing more difficult to take in hand, more perilous to conduct or more uncertain in its success than to take the lead in the introduction of a new order of things." Combining that cautionary with the Napoleonic stricture "L'audace, toujours l'audace" ("Boldness, always boldness"), he led a political *blitzkrieg,* which in the space of eighteen months demolished a statute that had been on the books for more than a century and was considered untouchable. But Lader knew that the governor of the state of New York, Nelson Rockefeller, a Republican reliably mesmerized by liberal causes, would not veto a bill striking down the abortion law of the state, and he might very well apply discreet pressure to those legislators who hung back on the issue.

One of Lader's greatest assets in this lightning campaign was also the most striking of the paradoxes in his personality. Though posing as a champion of the poor and powerless, he led a life of conspicuous affluence. Playing champion of the little people, a paradigmatic populist, he nursed a fine disdain for the common man. He often quoted to me the passage from Machiavelli that appeared to be his homing star:

> The people resemble a wild beast which, naturally
> fierce and accustomed to living in the woods, has

been brought up—as it were—in a prison and in servitude; and having by accident got its liberty, not being accustomed to search for its food and not knowing where to conceal itself, becomes the prey of the first who seeks to incarcerate it again.

It was, I think, this remorseless contempt for the egalitarian principles to which he paid such meticulous lip service that made it so easy for him to understand the Rockefellers and the other principalities and powers with whom he had to deal, and which made him so much more appealing and acceptable to the princes of this world than any genuine proletarian, or even any genuine sympathizer with the proletariat, could have been.

WHEN THE NEW STATUTE BECAME effective on July 1, 1970, I found myself beleaguered with new and increasingly demanding duties. Now that NARAL had shown the way, we were in demand to consult on political strategy and tactics with pro-abortion leaders in many other states. Further, having now achieved the law we had to make certain that it was not thrown into disrepute by clumsy practitioners little more adept than the illegals they would replace. In short, our greatest fear was that this unprecedented liberty might be jeopardized by a poor safety record. To that end I organized and staged a comprehensive symposium on abortion technique on July 1, 1970, at New York University Medical Center. Although only eighty doctors attended, we more than made up for the paucity of medical bodies by lavish coverage in the media.

Finally, because New York state became the abortion capital of the eastern half of the United States (California, with a similar, though not as permissive, law as ours, was drawing the abortion patients from the western half), we quickly discovered that abortion could not be done as a formal inpatient hospital procedure. There were simply too many to be done, and if we continued to admit every abortion patient to a hospital bed, or perform every abortion in a legitimate operating room, every willing hospital in the city would be flooded with abortion patients and even major university teaching hospitals would quickly be converted into abortion sanitaria.

An outpatient ambulatory procedure had to be devised to save the hospitals from sinking beneath the weight of all the abortion patients crowding into our waiting rooms. At St. Luke's Women's Hospital, with the aid of Dr. Harold Tovell, then the director of obstetrics and gynecology, and Avril Lawrence, the supervisor of the operating room, we devised an outpatient, walk-in, walk-out-three-hours-later program that worked efficiently and safely for our first-trimester patients. Women seeking late abortions (after thirteen to fourteen weeks) still had to be hospitalized, since the procedures we used were more complex and dangerous.

Another of my duties as chairman of the Medical Committee of NARAL (I was also a member of the Executive Committee) was to inspect the existing abortion clinics in the area and pass on their safety and medical effectiveness. At the time, I was also the senior member of a very busy three-person obstetrical and gynecological group practicing at St. Luke's Women's Hospital as well as at the Hospital for Joint Diseases (where I was chief of the gynecology service). My days (and nights) were filled to capacity. At no time—not even when I was the director of the Center for Reproductive and Sexual Health, the largest abortion clinic in the western world—did I give up (or even reduce) my obstetrical practice. In short, I was busy chasing my tail all over the city of New York and giving short shrift to my four-year-old son, Joseph. It is this last delinquency, this perversion of priorities, that I regret most deeply, now, twenty-five years later. That, and a seemingly invincible ignorance of the One who was offering me my life and my choices—which I invariably made incorrectly.

CHAPTER 8

The Procedure

ATTEMPTS TO CONTROL POPULATION growth by abortion can be traced to the mists of antiquity. As far back as the year 2737 B.C., the Emperor Shen Yung is said to have devised a prescription for the production of abortion. Taussig, in his encyclopedic work *Abortion, Spontaneous and Induced,* states that the practice is nearly as old as the social life of man. In the Ebers papyrus the Egyptians expatiate on the production of abortion with drugs and herbs. Moissides in 1922 published a monograph of 112 pages that enumerated all the various herbal and chemical agents used by the ancient Greek culture for the purpose. The Romans, despite a closetful of purported effective pharmacopeia, relied more on magic and incantation for practical purposes. Devereux, in his comprehensive survey of abortifacients used by primitive peoples the world over, has adumbrated a lengthy list of such agents, ranging from camel sputum to the chopped tail hairs of the deer: The Taulipang tribe used a paste of the Toncadira ant. The Masai employed an emulsion of goat dung. The Mescalero Apaches used a drug extracted from fermented vegetables. The Manja allowed a paste of crushed seeds to sprout, then offered the stems to the pregnant woman. In New Caledonia, green bananas were boiled into a hot soup, then drunk, while the Jivara peoples ate a raw egg for the same purpose.

In the eighteenth and nineteenth centuries, emmenagogues (drugs to restore an "obstructed" menstrual period) were in wide use and contained substances ranging from the relatively benign aloes (really a mild laxative), oils of pennyroyal, tansy, and juniper, to the more powerful ergot alkaloids and black hellebore, to the dangerous heavy metal compounds (lead, cadmium, and selenium) and tissue poisons such as podophyllin. Homing in on the current state of knowledge of labor and the hormones upon which it is dependent, Knaus accomplished abortion in rabbits with the injection of pituitary extract (the pituitary gland, at the base of the mid-brain, contains substances having the ability to force the uterus to contract, expelling the products of conception), but the cocktail he devised was not reliably effective in humans.

In the middle of the twentieth century, attention was focused on the potent new chemical tissue poisons that had been designed to treat cancer and allied disorders. Perhaps the most effective with respect to its abortifacient properties is the drug Methotrexate, manufactured and distributed by the Lederle Company. The drug is officially classified as an antimetabolite, i.e., a substance that interferes with the vital functions of folic acid in the life of the cell. The drug is especially toxic to the bone marrow (where the red and white blood cells are produced) and to trophoblastic tissue (pregnancy cells). It has many serious—even fatal—side effects, such as:

(a) a drastic reduction in the white blood cell count, impairing the immune system and leaving the patient helpless to combat even the most superficial infection;

(b) liver toxicity, which can be so severe as to kill the patient;

(c) kidney damage, ranging from mild disorders of kidney function to complete kidney shutdown and death;

(d) lung impairment, running the gamut from mild cough and breathlessness to fatal damage; and

(e) neurologic (nervous system) effects ranging from temporary behavioral abnormalities and abnormal reflexes to dissolution of brain tissue (leukoencephalopathy) and death.

Clearly, this is a drug to be used with extreme caution, and only by those physicians specially trained in its use and in the methods of recognizing early and treating vigorously its side effects.

One other listed side effect of the drug is toxicity to a pregnancy. Although it may cause abortion in some, other pregnancies will resist the abortifacient effect of the drug and the pregnancy will continue, often to result in the delivery of a grotesquely malformed child. On the plus side, the drug has saved the lives of many women who have been afflicted with a rare malignancy of pregnancy tissue called choriocarcinoma, which, before the introduction of Methotrexate, carried with it a 100 percent fatality rate but is now eminently curable with this drug.

Despite the exceedingly hazardous risks of this drug, it is now rapidly becoming the treatment of choice for ectopic pregnancy (pregnancy implanted in sites other than the womb, e.g., the fallopian tube, the cervix, the ovary, or the abdominal cavity), rapidly replacing the surgical treatment for such pregnancies, though it has never been approved by the Food and Drug Administration (FDA) for this purpose.

Recently, a family of drugs has been designed specifically to bring about abortion in the normally implanted, flourishing pregnancy. The drug RU-486 was designed in 1980 by a chemist, Georges Teutsch, while working for the German-owned French pharmaceutical company Roussel-Uclaf. It is a progesterone antagonist; i.e., it so resembles the hormone progesterone (which is manufactured in the female ovary in large amounts during pregnancy and upon which the pregnancy depends for its survival) that it is taken up by the pregnancy cells preferentially. RU-486, however, has no beneficial effects upon the pregnancy but acts to block the cell receptors for the vital *true* progesterone. It is as if one used a slightly faulty key to try to open a door and the faulty key broke off in the lock so the proper key could not be inserted.

RU-486 and its clones have had a short but inglorious history. The drug is reliably dependable to produce abortion only up to the ninth week of pregnancy, and even then is only 95 percent effective. The remaining 5 percent of women who have taken the drug either expel part of the pregnancy but continue to bleed and require a conventional suction evacuation or elect to carry the pregnancy to term with the potential for the delivery of a seriously malformed child. The drug, which is currently being used all over Europe and China and is undergoing "field tests" here in the United States, has caused the deaths of at least two women. Because it acts on the reproductive system of women, it has the potential to alter or influence in a yet-undefined but probably adverse manner the offspring of succeeding generations. Further, RU-486 is not reliably effective when taken by itself; forty-eight hours following its ingestion, the pregnant woman must then take another drug (misoprostol, a prostaglandin) to promote expulsion of the now-dead baby.

Misoprostol itself has an impressive list of undesirable and even dangerous side effects.

Extravagant claims have been made regarding other uses of RU-486. It has been touted as being useful in the treatment of breast cancer (it is not), meningioma (a rare variety of brain tumor), Cushing's syndrome (a disorder of the pituitary gland), depression, hypertension, Alzheimer's disease, glaucoma, post-term pregnancy, and severe wounds and burns. In short, its pro-abortion advocates have promoted the drug as a useful agent in the therapy of conditions and procedures unrelated to abortion, principally to distract the public attention from the drug's only proven, reliable function: abortion.

The Institute on Women and Technology is an organization dedicated to analyzing the effects of new and existing technologies on women, bringing a feminist perspective to public policy on specific technology and technology-based issues, and advocating technologies that empower women and sustain the natural world. The institute is based in Cambridge, Massachusetts, and is headed by three feminists, two of whom are schooled in biomedical issues (the third is an ethicist). The institute, in 1991, after reviewing the existing medical literature on RU-486 and after having interviewed women who have been given the drug, published a scathing critique of the drug. The report indicated that far from transforming abortion into a safe and private experience a woman can perform for herself (always the promise of "morning-after" pills), RU-486 requires five separate trips to the abortion clinic, two ultrasound examinations, a waiting period between the administration of the RU-486 and the prostaglandin to expel the dead fetus, plus an unpredictable interval between the giving of the drug and the actual abortion; the terror of severe bleeding and cramping at home prior to the expulsion of the dead fetus, and the not-infrequent failure of the drug to produce abortion, in turn requiring conventional dilation and curettage (D & C) by suction. (As the institute put it, "double abortion jeopardy.") Their conclusion: "No procedure requiring strict medical supervision and involving a host of risks and complications will help provide sexual and reproductive self-determination for women."

Surgical methods (suction curettage, and dilation and evacuation—D & E) remain by far the most widely used abortion techniques in the United States. Close to 90 percent of the 1.5 million abortions performed annually are done in the first trimester of the pregnancy, i.e., within the first thirteen weeks, and are done by the suction method; the remainder (late abortions) are done by D & E, although a rapidly shrinking number are still performed by an instillation method. The latter method is generally reserved for abortions after eighteen weeks, and requires the penetration of the pregnant uterus with a long hypodermic needle and the replacement of a portion of the amniotic fluid by a saline or urea solution. The cervix is dilated with laminaria (thin sticks of Japanese seaweed or similar strips of material impregnated with a hydrophilic material that soak up the watery secretions within the cervix, expand and thus dilate the cervix), then the saline or urea solution will cause the death of the fetus and initiate a minilabor. Once the fetus is dead or the minilabor begins, the patient is taken into a procedure room and a D & E completes the job.

The D & E is performed by breaking the bag of water with a pointed instrument thrust through the partly dilated cervix, then inserting grasping-and-tearing instruments into the womb. The fetus is then quartered, the torso isolated and disemboweled. The head is crushed and extracted in pieces. The placenta is located and scraped off the wall of the womb. This completes the procedure save for the abortionist reassembling all the removed parts on a side table adjoining the operating table. The fetus must be reconstructed to verify that all the vital parts have been removed with nothing of significance left within the womb to perpetuate bleeding and or become infected. Such late abortions—by whatever means—are no small matters surgically and carry a death rate equal to or exceeding that associated with childbirth at term.

In the case of early abortion in the first trimester, the classic D & C was in use until the mid-sixties. In this method the cervix was forcibly dilated with metal instruments to allow the insertion into the womb of a curette, a long metal instrument with a sharp-edged steel loop at the end. The curette was then used to scrape the pregnancy off the wall of the womb. This method carried with it the risk of thrusting the sharp instrument through the wall of the womb (perforation) or scraping the wall of the womb too vigorously, resulting in serious injury to the delicate lining and muscular inner layers of the womb (intrauterine synechiae or what is commonly known as Asherman's syndrome), which in turn produced grave disruption of the normal menstrual cycle or sterility.

In one of those curious and inexplicable syzygies of advanced technology with a sea change in social attitudes, the suction method of early abortion arrived on the scene at the exact historical moment it was most needed: the mid-sixties, when laws restricting abortion were about to fall en masse. Actually, vacuum suctioning of the pregnant uterus was first performed by a physician named Bykov in 1927; his device required the manual creation of a vacuum in order to "hoover out" the womb. It was not until the mid-thirties that an electrical apparatus was designed to create the vacuum quickly and effortlessly. By 1958 the Chinese had worked out the technique of suction curettage of the pregnant uterus on a mass scale; the method was soon introduced into the Soviet medical system in 1961, and by the mid-sixties reports of large numbers of abortions by this method were appearing in the medical literature from Israel and Sweden. Kerslake and Casey reported the first large series conducted in this country, and the rest is history.

Mass-scale efficient abortion technology had joined hands with the prevailing *zeitgeist* to make possible the assembly-line abortion clinics so desperately needed to free the hospitals to carry on their conventional duties. In March 1971, I myself had already reported a series of 645 abortions done by the suction method at Woman's Hospital, and I was entirely satisfied that this was the missing link in the technological chain. We had worked out the ambulatory approach to the procedure; we had ascertained that a simple local anesthesia administered by the abortionist around the cervix was sufficient to control the most painful portion of the procedure (the dilation of the cervix); we now possessed the rapid, safe, and efficient method of terminating the pregnancy; and we certainly had a huge built-in constituency awaiting for the word from us. The New York state law allowing abortion up through the twenty-fourth week of pregnancy would soon be replaced by *Roe v. Wade* which, despite some window dressing about the states' right to restrict abortion in the third trimester, would effectively permit abortion until labor. All that was missing now, in 1970, was the administrative skill to put the mass-scale extermination technology into practice.

As it turned out, that was my greatest triumph and my downfall.

CHAPTER 9

The Abortionist

CUT TO HORACE HALE HARVEY III and Barbara Pyle, a pair of hogarthian exotics so swollen with messianic zeal (and not a little collegial venality) that in those early days they stood front and center on the increasingly crowded stage of ditsy, sordid, feckless characters populating the abortion scene. Horace Hale Harvey III was a physician from New Orleans who had along the educational way earned a doctorate in Philosophy (he had written his thesis on decision making, although he himself was utterly incapable of making a decision even in the most urgent circumstance). He had had a rather undistinguished career in the practice of medicine in New Orleans. But he had performed a large number of abortions on pregnant women referred to him by the Rev. Howard Moody and his Clergy Consultation Referral Service (a sizable group of Protestant ministers and Jewish rabbis joined at the hip by a common disdain for restrictive abortion laws). He had endeared himself to Moody and his cohorts by charging as little as $300 for a first-trimester abortion at a time when other equally skilled abortionists were demanding $500 to $1,000 for the illegal operation. His complication rate was said to have been low. And if one of his patients suffered serious medical consequences, he would cover the patient's hospital bill out of his own pocket—an innovation that he carried over into the clinic he established in New York City and a custom that I subsequently maintained during my tenure as director of that clinic.

Barbara Pyle was a short, pudgy, and freckled but not unattractive Okie who had collided with Harvey at Tulane. He was working on his doctorate at the time, while she was in the undergraduate school. They shared a common interest—not to say obsession—in the matter of abortion and such related matters as sex education, contraceptive technology, and limiting population growth, and it was not long before they joined forces. When the old New York abortion statute fell in April 1970, Moody prevailed on Harvey and Pyle to set up shop in New York City, promising that his Clergy Consultation Referral Service could guarantee an unceasing flow of women from the entire eastern half of the United States. Harvey and Pyle mulled the offer, with Pyle of course making the ultimate decision to move, while Harvey was still dithering. She packed several station wagons and pick-up trucks full of medical gear, and they set out for New York in June. By July 1, 1970—the date upon which the new abortion statute went into effect—they had rented several suites of doctors' offices in a picturesque converted townhouse on Manhattan's upper east side and were open for business.

Business boomed. In six months the clinic—officially known as the Center for Reproductive and Sexual Health, but commonly known as Women's Services—increased its daily count of abortions from 10 to 120. The clinic had taken over the entire fifth floor of the office building and established an affiliation with a laboratory at which the patients would have their pre-abortion blood and urine tests done. Revenue was flooding into the coffers in such large amounts that Pyle was investing the profits in large-denomination U.S. government bonds. Women's Services, however, was a nonprofit clinic: No one had any equity, and all employees and management personnel (except the physicians, who were independent contractors) were salaried. The entire operation was presided over by Moody and his maverick band of ministers and rabbis. (Later, during my hegemony, there would be a board of trustees to whom I reported directly.)

Yet, there were a few insects in the unguent. For one, Dr. Harvey had neglected to obtain a license to practice medicine in the state of New York; this became known to the authorities by December 1970. Further, the counselors (young women who counseled the patients before the abortion, then accompanied the patients into the operating room as nurses though few actually were nurses), dissatisfied with their compensation of $50 per eight-hour shift, were agitating to join Local 1199, the union of hospital and health workers in New York City—a move Pyle and Harvey fought with true zeal. The counselors were largely young radicalized college-educated women who were unapologetically feminist and regarded the largely male physician staff as the enemy. This attitude did not make for harmonious relations in the clinic, especially as the quality of the physician staff was—in a word—deplorable, consisting of an extraordinary variety of drunks, druggies, sadists, sexual molesters, just plain incompetents, and medical losers. At least one was a fugitive from justice, with the FBI close on his tail.

By the end of January 1971, the state of New York had prepared a temporary injunction to be served on the clinic, which
would have effectively terminated the entire operation. With
the service of the injunction only days away, Howard Moody
telephoned me at home and pleaded with me to take over the
post of director at the clinic, stave off the injunction, clean up
the operation to enable the clinic to pass a searching inspection
by state health authorities, and ultimately obtain an operating
license from the state. With considerable reluctance and even
greater foreboding, I assented. I took over directorship of the
clinic on January 31, 1971.

My experiences in carrying out the mission assigned to me
by Howard Moody have been detailed elsewhere and I do not
intend to relive that nightmarish episode yet again in these
pages. Let it suffice to say that I accomplished my mission in a
dedicated and honorable fashion; I attended to my duties at that
clinic very early in the mornings, late at night, and over the
weekends so as to preserve the vast bulk of my working hours
for my group practice of obstetrics and gynecology. I quickly
learned to delegate quotidian responsibilities at the clinic to a
physician whom I admired and trusted, Dr. Jesse Blumenthal.
By keeping myself distanced from the daily operation of the
facility, i.e., I myself never performed an abortion there, I
engendered a certain respect even from the fractious counselor
group. I dealt with the personnel in an evenhanded manner,
participated in the labor negotiations with Local 1199 (the
clinic counselors *did* finally go union), and hired and fired
physicians until I had a clean, competent, industrious medical
staff. Within six months, we had secured an operating license
from New York state, which made Women's Services only the
second abortion clinic officially recognized by the state. The

first was a tiny facility in Syracuse operated by Dr. Jefferson Penfield, a friend of mine whom I had helped train in obstetrics and gynecology at New York Hospital.

As I look back across the twenty-five years separating me from that revolting extravaganza playing itself out on the bodies of pregnant women and their slaughtered babies, I am struck by the uncritical nature of the task we had set for ourselves, by the moral and spiritual vacuum at the core of this fantastic operation, by our unquestioned certainty of the high level of moral rectitude on which we operated. And yet, the thing was so obviously sordid. Why couldn't we make the link between the ethical and the moral, between the shoddy practices and shabby practitioners, the evident greed and callous motives, between the crassness of the enterprise and those involved in it, between all these ethical indicators and the grotesque immorality of the act itself? St. Thomas teaches that God has given it to us to apprehend Being under each of its four transcendental aspects: the Good, the True, the Beautiful, and the Oneness. The apprehension of each aspect helps us to uncover the others so that we can apprehend, for instance, the Truth by its Goodness, or the Good by its Beauty. Why could we not triangulate from the shoddy to the shameful?

The physicians, who performed ten or fifteen abortions daily, were paid at the rate of $70 to $90 per hour. One obstetrician-gynecologist would practice his specialty in Lexington, Kentucky, from Monday to Friday, then fly up to New York City, work five shifts of eight hours each at the clinic over the weekend, and then fly back to resume his practice on Monday morning. He earned $185,000 in the one year he worked at the clinic.

The abortionists were required by the protocol I had worked out to examine with the naked eye the contents in the gauze bag that hung from the end of the suction apparatus, checking to see that the appropriate amount of fetal parts were present. They would thus personally examine the remains of perhaps a dozen abortions every workday. At the conclusion of their eight-hour shift, they would return home to their families, to their practices, to their houses of worship. (Many of the non-Jewish physicians were churchgoers; the Jewish physicians were for the most part either Reform Jews or atheists, as was I.)

Robert Lifton, a psychiatrist, examined the behavior of Nazi doctors who presided over the mass slaughter in the camps and then returned to ordinary family life at the end of the working day. He termed this phenomenon "doubling," the division of the self into two functioning wholes. The physicians I inherited when I took over the directorship of the clinic may not have required such subtle psychological self-protection. They were a professional press gang mercifully unburdened with ethical or moral baggage. Dr. Eliezar Schkolnik, a short, paunchy, middle-aged voluble Russian, epitomized the vulturous scavengers who preyed on the abortion revolution in its earliest day. Besides working in our clinic, he also was on the staff of an abortion clinic functioning in the same building two floors below, and if there were a lull in activities at Women's Services, Schkolnik would steal down the two flights of stairs and nonchalantly report for work in the other clinic, capitalizing on the fact that in those first heady days of the abortion liberty there were few physicians willing to work in such facilities. When I learned of his split-level performance, I immediately decided to fire him— though he was an accomplished technician and could bring off the most difficult abortions without even breaking a sweat.

Happily he quietly faded away, and by the end of the second week of my administration he was no longer to be seen in our clinic. He surfaced again several years later as the director of a small abortion clinic so filthy and so disreputable that health care investigators of the state of New York sent in a female decoy to his clinic armed with a specimen of male urine. He had it tested in what laughingly passed for his laboratory and reported to her after a decent interval, perhaps three minutes, that she was indeed pregnant and he would be happy to do the abortion. For this and assorted other medical and moral transgressions, his license to practice medicine was revoked by New York state in 1976. In 1980, his body was found lying in an obscure alleyway in Brooklyn, a single bullet hole behind the left ear.

As I say, however, I was able in those days at least to replace the Schkolniks. With a combination of money and an appeal to political duty, I soon put together a staff of physicians of which any major hospital would have been proud: conscientious, careful, decent physicians dedicated to their task with little or no internal dissension, and unimpaired by ethical qualms.

But the core question keeps intruding itself on my consciousness, even twenty-five years later: I had replaced a gaggle of medical rogues and ruffians with a spotless, respectable collection of superbly trained, highly competent physicians—and these new recruits continued to carry out the same grisly task with no medical indication or excuse at all. The rusting, failing medical machinery had been replaced with a shiny, new, massive apparatus—but the morality of what we were engaged in was altogether unchanged.

They had all taken the same Hippocratic Oath as I had; all supposedly been inculcated with reverence for life. Some, like me, were the sons of physicians and had been brought up in the same medically virtuous climate that I had been. It is not difficult to understand why the Schkolniks of the medical world would flock to feed on the abortion liberty; but why were these medically successful, technically superior physicians willing to continue the very same unspeakable project that their medical inferiors had commenced?

Doctors subject themselves to a lengthy period of higher education and technical training. They learn to diagnose the illnesses of mind and body, and bring to bear on those who are ill the specialized technical training in which they are certified. In the performance of these services they are compensated by payment in currency, by special recognition from their peers, by acclaim of the nonmedical community, and, perhaps greatest of all, by the intoxicating flush of potency that attends the sacred privilege of invading another's body with moral sanction and legal impunity.

The minimal description of a doctor then is this: a highly trained technician, daily exposed to exceptionally powerful material and spiritual temptations. It has been my experience that only those who have an inflexible inner spiritual column supporting the immense weight of medical obligations and responsibilities survive intact the lure of the worldly temptations in the medical world: the uninterrupted flow of money, the drumfire of flattery, and the inebriating effects of special privilege. It is no accident that great early physicians and scientists were deeply spiritual: Hippocrates swore his oath to his gods; Aristotle (perhaps the greatest empirical scientist of all time) revered the idea of God as the Prime Mover; Claudius Galen, who built upon the work of Aristotle and Hippocrates, early on declared himself a monotheist and was cherished by Arabic and Hebrew physicians who followed in his wake; and Rabbi Moses ben Maimon (Maimonides), a codifier of the Talmud, was a talented physician to the court of Saladin in

Egypt and wrote the *Guide for the Perplexed,* which strove to marry the elements of spirituality with the science of medicine. William Harvey, the discoverer of the circulation of blood, was convinced of the existence of a Supreme Creative Intelligence and practiced his Protestant religion zealously. Without such an absolute guide to virtue, doctors, exposed as they are to greater temptations than most, are likely to fall further.

It remains true, however, that abortionists even today, more than two decades into the history of abortion on demand in America, do tend to come from the lower orders of the medical profession. In fact, that may be more true than it was in the early 1970s.

In May 1991, a public citizen health research group published a report titled *9479 Questionable Doctors.* This group persuaded the Medical boards of forty-one states and the District of Columbia to provide it with a list of all physicians disciplined since the beginning of 1985. It obtained similar information from the Inspector-General's Office of the U.S. Department of Health and Human Services and the Food and Drug Administration, and also notices from the Federal Registrar of doctors and dentists whose privileges to prescribe controlled substances were revoked, restricted, or denied.

In toto, the doctors listed had incurred twenty-three types of disciplinary actions, ranging from license revocation to private reprimand; committed sixteen different categories of offenses, from criminal convictions to altering patient records; and incurred thirty-two different types of professional misconduct charges, including "procuring a criminal abortion" (whatever *that* means under *Roe v. Wade*), "engaging in lewd conduct," and "sexual abuse of a person other than a patient, or of an unspecified person."

The report reached the sobering conclusion that the nation's system for protecting the public from medical incompetence and malfeasance is still far from adequate, and in fact only in a few states do medical boards actively seek to uncover bad physicians, or even those who have been disciplined in other states, before receiving complaints, in order to prevent misconduct and poor care. Many sanctioned doctors are repeat offenders or had been sanctioned in more than one state. The report contends that far "too little discipline is still being done" and that only a small percentage of doctors who harm their patients face state sanctions.

IN QUEENS COUNTY, NEW YORK, a thirty-three-year-old woman died in a botched abortion at the hands of Dr. David Benjamin (also known as Elyias Bonrouhi). How did she come into his hands?

Dr. Benjamin had been barred from surgical privileges at St. Elizabeth's Hospital in Utica, New York. According to Anthony Dardano, M.D., former chief and now vice chairman of the Department of Obstetrics and Gynecology at that hospital: "He didn't even meet what I would consider the bare minimum standard of care." In 1985, Benjamin was charged with operating without an anesthetic, attempting complicated deliveries in his office (he was unable to obtain hospital privileges), and sewing the wrong parts of a woman's anatomy together after an operation. These charges resulted in a slap on the wrist—a three-month suspension of his license in 1986. He then surfaced in 1993 in Corona, Queens, performed a second-trimester abortion in his office, and managed to cause the woman's death in the course of the abortion. Mercifully, his New York state license was finally revoked.

Dr. Stephen Brigham was proclaimed a hero when he volunteered to replace Dr. John Britton, the abortionist who was murdered by Paul Hill in July 1994 in Pensacola. There can be no doubt that the murder of Dr. Britton was a heinous act. Doubts, however, are very much in order about Dr. Brigham, who grandly announced he would bare his bosom to rogue assassins and other assorted murderous types in service of his ideals. Dr. Brigham, it turns out, had already had his medical license suspended in New York state and was charged with negligence and incompetence in his treatment of two women from New Jersey and one from Pennsylvania on whom he was paid to perform second-trimester abortions. He allegedly perforated the uterus of one of the New Jersey women who was twenty-four weeks pregnant and injured not only her uterus but also her colon. The other New Jersey woman, who was twenty-six weeks pregnant, simply suffered a laceration of the cervix, which he allegedly failed to recognize and suture. She had suffered such massive blood loss by the time she was admitted to the hospital that she required a hysterectomy.

Prior to Brigham's braggadocio, one Dr. Allen Kline had stepped manfully into the breach to replace the murdered Dr. Britton. He donned a bulletproof vest, flanked himself with a police escort, and strode through the front doors of the Pensacola Women's Medical Services abortion clinic, proclaiming that he was determined to continue the heroic work of the decedent physician in providing "reproductive services" for those in crisis as a result of an unplanned pregnancy. Unfortunately for the patient population in Pensacola, the selfsame Dr. Kline had presided over the abortion of thirteen-year-old Dawn Ravenell at twenty-one weeks' gestation at the Eastern Women's Medical Center abortion clinic in New York City.

That procedure culminated in the coma and death of the little girl. In the malpractice litigation that followed, the child's family was awarded $1.3 million in damages. The jury found the callous negligence and indifference to human life so egregious that they termed the incident an "abomination." Incidentally, court records indicate that the Eastern Women's Medical Center had fabricated and altered its medical records in an attempt to cover up the tragedy.

In November 1991, Dr. Robert Crist performed an abortion on a seventeen-year-old girl. She bled profusely after the operation and was rushed to Ben Taub Hospital in Houston, where she died on the same day. She was twenty-two weeks pregnant. Dr. Crist had been involved in two other disastrous cases. A retarded woman in St. Louis expired two days after he performed an abortion on her, and a Texas woman claimed she delivered a mutilated baby several days after Crist performed an abortion on her. (These two cases were reported in detail in the *Kansas City Star*—Crist insists that the claims were dismissed.)

Dr. Milan Chepko was indicted by a federal grand jury in 1989 for mailing and distributing videotapes of children engaged in sex acts (oral and anal). He was charged with two counts of interstate transportation of videotapes that involved the sexual exploitation of children. If convicted on all counts, he faced thirty years in prison and $1.5 million in fines. Dr. Chepko had confined his professional duties to working in two abortion clinics in Mississippi.

Dr. Ming Kow Hah, who practiced in Elmhurst, New York, in 1990, was accused of a botched abortion and had his medical license suspended by state Health Commissioner David Axelrod, who termed him "an imminent danger to the health of the people of this state." The botched abortion resulted in a hysterectomy and repair of other extensive internal injuries. Dr. Hah, evidently not easily dissuaded from his vocation, had previously had his medical license revoked in Michigan in 1975, and his Illinois license revoked in 1978.

In January 1993, Angela Sanchez, twenty-seven, was found dead after having been given an injection at the Clinica Femenina de la Communidad, an abortion clinic in Orange County (California); she was said to have been pregnant. The clinic owner, Alicia Ruiz Hanna, was arrested and booked into Orange County jail on suspicion of murder. Hanna claimed to be a registered nurse, but state agencies denied that Hanna had been licensed in the state of California.

The undisputed leader of the pack of abortion hyenas, however, is Dr. Abu Hayat, a sixty-one-year-old graduate of Calcutta Medical School and a former major in the U.S. Army Medical Corps. He was issued a license to practice medicine in the state of New York on September 6, 1973, and his license remained valid until the macabre series of incidents in question. Hayat operated his abortion mill with the fine regard for utter secrecy and magical indirection one would expect in a CIA operative fomenting a revolution in Central America: He would advertise his services in the Spanish-language newspaper *El Diario* and have the pregnant women report to a storefront office in Brooklyn. They would then be brought (he evidently did not think it necessary to blindfold them, although had he done so a few might have deserted the operation in pure terror and thus saved themselves from the odious machinations of this monster) to his office on Avenue A and Ninth Street, on the lower east side of Manhattan. It was at this site that the professional incompetence, the colossal venality, and the conscienceless perfect evil of the man exhibited themselves.

A series of hearings conducted by the New York State Department of Health were held to discuss the professional misconduct of Dr. Hayat. The hearings took place on December 3, 4, and 17, 1991. Hayat disdained to appear at any of these hearings. In the course of the hearings, it was brought out that a woman named Rosa Rodriguez went to Hayat's storefront office at 296 Broadway in Brooklyn on October 25, 1991. She thought herself to be three to four months pregnant and in response to Hayat's advertisement in *El Diario* had decided to have the pregnancy terminated. She was whisked by two of Hayat's employees to the Ninth Street abortion mill in Manhattan, where she was told the abortion would cost $1,500. She indicated that she only had $1,000 in cash with her. Hayat accepted her passport, her residency green card, and a gold and diamond ring as collateral against the outstanding balance of $500. He then examined her, anesthetized her, and inserted laminaria into her cervix in an effort to accomplish dilation of the cervix sufficient to carry out the abortion the next day. When she awakened he instructed her to return home, and to report to his Brooklyn office the next day. She did so, and again was whisked to the Manhattan abortion chamber by one of his employees.

At this point, however, Rodriguez informed Dr. Hayat that she did *not* wish to proceed with the abortion and that he should please remove the laminaria from her cervix. This is a perfectly safe procedure medically. Generally, the pregnancy will proceed uneventfully once the laminaria are removed, especially if they have only been present for twenty-four hours. Dr. Hayat, however, coldly informed her that she had *no* choice but to proceed with the abortion. He gave her an injection that tranquilized her, and when she had awakened he informed her that he had removed the "old medication [the original laminaria]" and had replaced them with others. He then instructed her to return to his Manhattan office the next day, but under no circumstances was she to call or report to a hospital—if she experienced any adverse effects she was to call one of the employees at his Brooklyn office.

Rodriguez, however, was not three or four months pregnant but in her thirty-second week. That night, October 26, 1991, she began to experience severe abdominal pain and labor contractions. She had had a child three-and-a-half years earlier and was familiar with labor pains. Rodriguez then called—as instructed—the employees at the Brooklyn office, who in turn put her in touch with Dr. Hayat. He told her she was not yet "ready" and should wait until the next day. She was in such excruciating pain by this time that she called the Brooklyn office employee, who instructed her to come over to her house where she would be taken care of. She declined the invitation, informed her mother of all that had been going on, and was taken by ambulance to the Jamaica Hospital where, in the emergency room, she delivered a fourteen-hundred-gram (just a little over three pounds) living female infant with the right arm missing. Rather than "replacing" the "old medication," Dr. Hayat had in fact begun the abortion. He had ruptured her bag of waters, and begun dismembering the child by twisting off her arm. When he realized the extent of the pregnancy (he had never troubled himself to obtain an ultrasound examination before the attempted abortion to ascertain with certainty how far along the pregnancy was), he awakened Rodriguez and callously dismissed her from his charge, relying on local emergency medical facilities to provide a satisfactory solution to the matter. The child to this day is perfectly healthy but is missing her right arm.

As the New York State Department of Health and the media began to probe deeper into Hayat's career, other incidents came to light. In March 1991, he had begun a second-trimester abortion on a woman but during the course of the abortion he left the patient, met the husband downstairs in the waiting room, informed him that the pregnancy was more advanced than he had thought (again, he had not bothered with a preoperative ultrasound examination), and demanded an additional $500 from the husband. He told the husband that if he did not hand over the $500 immediately he would have to terminate the procedure in the midst of the most hazardous part of the operation and send the patient home. The husband indicated that he did not have the money with him but would be sure to have it the following afternoon. This was not satisfactory with Dr. Hayat. He threw the patient and her husband out of his abortion mill while she was still bleeding heavily and under sedation. She ended up at St. Luke's Hospital in New York City, where she was treated for massive sepsis and blood loss. The abortion had to be completed at that facility.

In September 1990, Hayat began an abortion on a patient who evidenced brisk vaginal bleeding, severe abdominal pain, and difficulty breathing during the procedure. He hurriedly got her off his table and out of his facility. She ended up at King's County Medical Center in Brooklyn the next day with overwhelming sepsis and a disseminated intravascular coagulopathy (a life-threatening defect in the clotting systems of the blood). He had also perforated her uterus. She died of septic shock on September 26, 1990.

In July 1988, Hayat carried out an abortion on a woman who was seventeen weeks pregnant. Following the procedure she began to bleed heavily, but he told her that the bleeding was normal and that it was perfectly safe for her to go home. She remained in extreme pain, however, and two days later returned to his office where he carried out an additional unspecified procedure on her and then sent her home again. After being home twelve hours she began to pass stool through her vagina. She was rushed to North Central Bronx Hospital, where it was discovered that not only had Hayat perforated her uterus in the course of the abortion, but had also injured the large intestine (colon), creating a utero-colic fistula (an abnormal channel of communication between the uterus and the intestine). He had also neglected to remove some parts of the fetal skull, which were later found lying free in the patient's cervix.

And, oh yes, Hayat was also charged with sexually abusing a woman in the course of an abortion in October 1991. In total, an impressive record of venality, professional incompetence, and indifference to human life. In November 1991, the New York State Department of Health revoked his medical license, calling him "an imminent danger to the health of the people of New York state." In January 1993, Hayat was indicted by a grand jury on thirteen counts, ranging from causing serious injury to a baby (the Rodriguez child) to a depraved indifference to human life, to falsifying business records (he had altered his patient records in order to conceal his grisly practices). The trial went forward before Justice Jeffrey Atlas in Part 39 of the Criminal Term of the supreme court of the state of New York: Hayat never took the stand in his own defense and is now serving a term of nine and one-third years to twenty-seven and two-thirds years in an upstate New York prison.

Not all those who do abortions are medical monsters; nor are all medical monsters abortionists. Dr. Michael Swango, a resident in psychiatry at the University Hospital in Stonybrook,

New York, for instance, was suspended from his duties in October 1993 for concealing that he had once been convicted of poisoning his coworkers. Specifically, he had served two years in an Illinois prison for lacing fellow paramedics' food with ant poison. And in Wilmington, North Carolina, the medical license of Dr. Raymond Sattle, a neurosurgeon, was suspended in November 1994 because he left a patient's brain exposed for twenty-five minutes while he got lunch; he was also reprimanded for forgetting the names of surgical instruments he required during the operation, for ordering a nurse to drill holes in a patient's head and work on the outer brain even though she had no training to do so, and for ordering that intravenous fluids be administered to him (the surgeon) during the procedure because he felt as if he were about to pass out.

It may also be that media attention focuses more sharply on misadventures in the abortion trade because abortion itself is such a combustible issue. Nevertheless, consultation with major malpractice insurance carriers reveals that abortion is one of the three or four most frequently litigated malpractice actions in the United States, so much so that although a first-trimester abortion is a relatively undemanding technical procedure, the malpractice carriers classify it as "major surgery," and any physician who does abortions and wishes malpractice coverage must pay much higher rates than those who do comparably simple procedures.

MY OWN EXPERIENCE AT WOMEN'S SERVICES leads me to conclude that the abortionist problem is inherent to abortion and likely to get worse, not better. As I noted, my first task when I took over Women's Services was to rid the medical staff of all the medical and paramedical offal and reorganize the operation along the lines of a university teaching facility. In fact, we were hosts and instructors to many other reputable physicians and organizations who wished to set up a similar operation, including but not limited to the Planned Parenthood group. We published our statistics in prestigious medical journals such as the *New England Journal of Medicine* and the *American Journal of Obstetrics and Gynecology.* I published a series of articles in such journals and spoke at district meetings of the American College of Obstetrics and Gynecology (ACOG).

The result of this legitimizing process was, as any sound economist could have predicted, disastrous for the economic health of the physician staff. I reduced the pay scale of physicians doing the abortions to the point where we could offer abortions for $125 apiece, the Medicaid magic number, instead of the $200 scale that prevailed when I took over. We brought it within the range of the poorest and made the procedure so legitimate that the Medicaid system was finally persuaded to pay for those who lacked even the $125. Before I took over, physicians had been earning $75 per abortion, a scheme that resulted in multiple abuses, including doctors fighting over patients to work on and abjuring of difficult abortions since they took time to do. Initially, I placed the physicians on an hourly pay scale of $70 to $90 per hour (my own pay as director was $30,000/year).

As other clinics sprang up—many with competent, conscientious physicians on their staffs, at least at first—competition for the abortion dollar became more intense. Although we had a far-flung powerful referral mechanism through the Clergy Consultation Referral Service, which counted among its members twelve hundred ministers and rabbis over the eastern half of the United States, we were still in a fight for patients. Another clinic functioned two floors below us in the same building, and they were in the habit of sending "pullers" to the local airports to identify our clients and convince them that they represented our clinic (same address, after all) and then speed them to the *third* floor (we were on the fifth) for the abortion *and* the fee.

As competition intensified and assembly-line clinics cut costs, I was forced to reduce compensation for the doctors. With their pay being reduced, gynecologists trained to do major surgery in the female pelvis for considerable sums began to notice, after doing five thousand or ten thousand abortions under heavy pressure, that they were bored and underpaid, especially as their own private practices increased. Many of my best operatives resigned, to return full time to their own practices. Abortion clinics, my own included, were increasingly populated with younger, inexperienced physicians and—yet again—the medical losers.

Remember, legal abortion came on the scene just as other opportunities were opening up in the field of obstetrics and gynecology: assisted reproductive technology (in vitro fertilization and its offspring), more sophisticated obstetrics with ultrasound and electronic fetal heart monitoring, chemotherapy and radical surgery of gynecologic tumors, the proliferation of medical schools needing new personnel for teaching purposes, and the lavishing of government grants for clinical research in obstetrics and gynecology. These also were powerful factors that lured the competent away from abortion clinics, leaving the vacancies to the inexperienced and the losers.

Finally, and perhaps most important, there was a growing feeling, despite the frenzied politicking from feminist-dominated, politically correct professional organizations such as the ACOG, that abortion was a tedious, assembly-line, marginally respectable occupation that demanded little or nothing from the physician, technically or ethically: The pregnant woman was escorted into the operating room at the last minute after having been propped up in the decision-making area by zealous feminist "counselors." The doctor would introduce himself (if he were civilized enough to do so; many abortion victims have sworn they never were told the name of the doctor who mutilated them in the course of the botched abortion), examine them once they were under anesthesia, and then suction out the uterus—never to see the patient again.

Is this what the conscientious, dedicated OB-GYN had spent four years in college, four years in medical school, and at least four more years, seven years in my own case, in residency training to do? Where was the patient–doctor relationship here? Where was the "internal ethic of medicine" in this deadening landscape? Where were justice, veracity, promise-keeping, and avoidance of killing, all the key elements of normative medical ethics? Is it any wonder that flotsam and jetsam like Hayat, Benjamin, Brigham, Kline, and their ilk drifted to the scummy shores of abortion?

Dr. David Grimes, professor of obstetrics and gynecology at the University of Southern California School of Medicine in Los Angeles, recently published an article in the house organ of the ACOG in which he bemoaned the shortage of "abortion-providers" in the United States, and pointed out that 83 percent of counties in the United States have no identifiable "provider." Dr. Grimes has been in the vanguard of the pro-abortion movement: He functioned for many years in the Abortion Surveillance Project of the Centers for Disease Control in Atlanta,

Georgia, and was one of the early proponents of the D & E technique for second-trimester abortions. He is now engaged in pushing the RU-486 French abortion pill with nothing less than a messianic zeal. Grimes laments that, as of 1985 (the last comprehensive survey on the subject) the proportion of residency training programs offering special training in the performance of abortions had declined significantly. He attributes this decline to a combination of poor pay, low prestige, frequent harassment, suboptimal working conditions, and tedium. Grimes does not dwell on the ethical aspects of the procedure nor ask why this *particular operation* in the immensely broad spectrum of surgical procedures should be singled out for failure in contradistinction to the many other tedious procedures in modern medicine. In fairness, he does include "low prestige" in his list of "disincentives" to performing abortions, and I doubt it is an epistemic overstretch to venture that the deliberate destruction of a living, demonstrably human, being is a practice anathema to all but the most morally insouciant physicians, and can justifiably be described as bearing "low prestige" in the medical community.

Dr. Ralph W. Hale, now executive director of the ACOG, tries to explain the lack of OB-GYNs willing to do abortions by arguing that many older obstetricians are no longer doing abortions because their patient population has aged with them and are no longer in the reproductive years. To the contrary, it appears that it is younger OB-GYNs, trained in the era of ultrasound and with far more worthwhile endeavors open to them, who are leading the field away from abortion and leaving it to the quacks and hacks. In actual fact, as of 1991 only 12 percent of residency training programs required training in first-trimester abortions. Abortion is surgically unchallenging work that hardly fits within the classic bounds and aspirations of young physicians in training. Residents in obstetrical training programs have made it known to their mentors that they prefer not to waste their valuable training time carrying out a destructive procedure that—in any case—is now largely confined to the shadowy fringes of medical practice, i.e., the abortion mills.

AT THE TIME I WAS RUNNING THE CLINIC, I was simultaneously practicing obstetrics and gynecology, doing deliveries, and traveling all over the country lobbying legislatures and politicians to open up their laws (this was before *Roe v. Wade*). I was very busy. I hardly ever saw my family. I had a young son and a wife, but I was hardly ever at home. I bitterly regret those years, if for no other reason than that I failed to see my son grow up. I am immensely regretful of that, and my absence has led to serious problems with my son. I was also a pariah in the medical profession. I was known as the abortion king. My papers on abortion, eagerly received by the liberal press (and even the liberal medical press) did not make me popular with many in my profession. My practice dwindled because doctors would not send patients to me. (Now that I am pro-life, I am again exiled by the medical establishment—nobody speaks to me.) At the end of 1972, I was exhausted and wanted to leave the clinic. I resigned. After a brief power struggle, somebody else took over.

CHAPTER 10

The Vector of Life

WHEN I LEFT THE CLINIC and became chief of obstetrical services at St. Luke's Hospital, I had for the first time in years a little time and space to think. I am sure it was no coincidence— the hand of God was present—that at that very same time we began moving a marvelous new technology into the hospital. It was ultrasound, which for the first time threw open a window into the womb. We also began to observe the fetal heart on electronic fetal heart monitors. For the first time, I began to think about what we really had been doing at the clinic. Ultrasound opened up a new world. For the first time, we could really see the human fetus, measure it, observe it, watch it, and indeed bond with it and love it. I began to do that. Ultrasound pictures of the fetus have an incredibly strong impact on the viewer. A study in the *New England Journal of Medicine* provided evidence of how potent this technology is. About ten years ago, an article in the journal reported that when ten pregnant women came to an abortion clinic and were shown ultrasound pictures of the fetus before the abortion, only one went through with the abortion. Nine left the clinic pregnant. That is how powerful the bonding is. I found myself bonding with the unborn.

While I continued to do abortions for what seemed to me to be medically justified reasons, I no longer felt certain that abortion on demand was right. In 1974, I sat down and wrote an article for the *New England Journal of Medicine.* It was not a pro-life article, but in it I articulated my growing doubts and fears about what I had been doing. I made the flat statement that I had presided over sixty thousand deaths, and I said that the fetus is life. I said that it's a special order of life, but it's life, and we have to be reverent in the presence of any kind of life.

In that article, I obliquely asked many questions about why physicians sworn to uphold life performed abortions. I asked questions but provided few, if any, answers. I set forth the following propositions:

> There is no longer serious doubt in my mind that human life exists within the womb from the very onset of pregnancy, despite the fact that the nature of intrauterine life has been the subject of considerable dispute in the past.

This is a statement that now, twenty years later, must be amended because of the new information we have about genetics and assisted reproductive technology (in vitro fertilization and its scientific spawns). If I were writing today, I'd have to assert that human life begins even earlier, with the complex process of fertilization—a miracle in chemistry, physics, and molecular biology occurring within the fallopian tube. By the time the fertilized egg, dividing and beginning to organize itself, enters the womb, life has been in action for at least three days.

But I'm getting ahead of myself. In that same 1974 article, I also wrote:

> Life is an interdependent phenomenon for all of us. It is a continuous spectrum which begins in utero and ends in death—the bands of the spectrum are designated by words such as fetus, infant, child, adolescent and adult. We must courageously face the fact—finally—that human life of a special order is being taken [in the process of abortion], and since the vast majority of pregnancies are carried successfully to term, abortion must be seen as the interruption of a process which would otherwise have produced a citizen of the world. Denial of this reality is the crassest kind of moral evasiveness.

These were fairly modest assertions—hardly a wild-eyed prolifer on the loose here—but they released an incredible store of emotion. The response to that article, I am told by the *New England Journal of Medicine,* was the largest they have ever gotten—even up until today. They were deluged by mail, and, of course, they didn't bother with the letters—they sent them all to me. The postman delivered huge sacks of mail. These letters were not fan letters. They were coming from physicians who had excoriated me for being an abortionist four years earlier but now, as the abortion pie had grown and they were pulling in the money right and left, they had changed their minds. I was overwhelmed by the vituperation, the threats, and the phone calls. Threats were made against my life and my family. I thought to myself, well, I have really hit a nerve. I have got to think this out.

I continued to do abortions through 1976. I was doing abortions and delivering babies, but increasingly I found the moral tensions building and becoming intolerable. On one floor of the hospital we would be delivering babies and on another floor doing abortions. Because *Roe v. Wade* didn't set any restrictions, we could do abortions into the ninth month, before the first labor pain. At this writing, there are at least fifteen thousand abortions after the twenty-first week every year. Today, at twenty-one weeks, the baby is considered viable. These are not even abortions; they are murdering premature babies. In the mid-seventies, I would be up on one floor, putting the hypertonic saline into a woman twenty-three weeks pregnant, and on another floor down, I would have someone in labor at twenty-three weeks, and I would be trying to salvage this baby. The nurses were caught in the same bind, the same moral whipsaw. What were we doing here, were we saving babies or were we killing them?

I finally restricted my abortion practice to those who I judged to have a compelling need for an abortion. This was in the late seventies. I included rape and incest as compelling reasons. During this period, I wrote a book called *Aborting America*. In my book, I listed a lot of medical conditions that would justify abortion. I did two or three abortions in 1978, and then in 1979 I did my last one. I had come to the conclusion that there was no reason for an abortion at any time; this person in the womb is a living human being, and we could not continue to wage war against the most defenseless of human beings.

Having looked at the ultrasound, I could no longer go on as before. But this "conversion" was a purely empirical event. This amazing technology has allowed us to learn more about the fetus since its advent than in almost all the history of medicine before that time. In order to give you some idea of the immense influence of this new technology on the practice of obstetrics and our knowledge of the fetus, let me tell you that there is a huge book called *The Cumulative Index Medicus,* which lists every article published in every medical journal in the world. In the 1969 edition of the Index under the heading of "fetus, physiology and anatomy of," there were five articles in the world's literature. As recently as that, we knew almost nothing of the fetus; when abortion on demand was unleashed in the United States, fetology essentially did not exist. In 1979, there were twenty-eight hundred articles, and by 1994 there were close to five thousand. This technology had opened a new world to us.

Although he was writing three decades earlier about something too tiny to be seen with the naked eye, Dr. George W. Corner, the great endocrinologist and research scientist who first isolated and identified the vital female hormone progesterone, a hormone essential to the growth and development of the unborn child, seemed to realize that it was the hidden nature of human development that makes us undervalue it so tragically. His memorable description of fertilization, written in the 1940s, deserves to be quoted:

> The fertilization of an egg by the sperm is one of the greatest wonders of nature, an event in which magnificently small fragments of... life are driven by cosmic forces to their appointed end, the growth of a living human being. As a spectacle, it can be compared only with an eclipse of the sun, or the eruption of a volcano. It is in fact the most common and

nearest to us of nature's cataclysms, and yet it is very seldom observed because it occurs in a realm most people never see—the region of microscopic things.

After my exposure to ultrasound, I began to rethink the prenatal phase of life. Gradually, I began to understand that two hundred or three hundred years ago, childhood had not been understood as a special time in our lives and that in the seventeenth century, children as young as five years old were made to work in factories. There was no recognition of the phenomenon of childhood or of their needs until the last hundred or so years. Adolescence, adulthood, and senescence—they are all bands in the continuing spectrum of life. When I began to study fetology, it dawned on me, finally, that the prenatal nine months are just another band in the spectrum of life.

Ironically, these nine months may be the most important nine months in our lives. That's when our organs are forming, our brain is forming, and we experience our first sensory impressions. In the womb, we can distinguish one kind of music from another. I have put Mozart in a tape player and held it against a womb at, say, seven months, and the baby moved a little, but when I put Van Halen on, the baby was jumping all over the place. The first nine months are a learning time, a time when we are organizing ourselves. To disrupt or abort a life at this point is intolerable—it is a crime. I don't make any bones about using that word: Abortion is a crime.

What is the moral status of the fetus? If I consider abortion a crime, it stems from my notion of its moral status. What moral status is accorded to the fetus by those who believe that abortion is acceptable?

The crux of the issue as defined by most pro-abortion theorists is whether the embryo, or later the fetus, is to be considered a "person." It is crucial for them to move the debate onto that ground because there is simply no doubt that even the early embryo is a human being. All its genetic coding and all its features are indisputably human. As to being, there is no doubt that it exists, is alive, is self-directed, and is not the same being as the mother—and is therefore a unified whole.

So personhood must be made critical if abortion is to be moral. What then is a person?

One popular theory is explained by Bonnie Steinbok (who relies heavily on the work of Joel Feinberg) in a book titled *Life Before Birth: The Moral and Legal Status of Embryos and Fetuses.* She hews to the "interest view," which holds that the possession of interests is both necessary and sufficient—or, stated another way, that beings who have rights have moral status. A little circular, but let it go for a minute—we have bigger fish to fry. She dismisses out of hand Albert Schweitzer's ethic of the reverence for life, chiefly by consigning Schweitzer's aversion to breaking a beautiful crystal as confused and impractical. Then she segues into the idea of "conscious awareness" and, by implication, "personhood." Carved above the door of that edifice is the following:

> Only beings with interests can have claims against moral agents. Interests are compounded out of beliefs, aims, goals, concerns. Biological life alone does not endow a being with interests. Permanently non-sentient non-conscious beings cannot have interests. Without interests, they cannot have moral status.

There are serious flaws, however, in defining moral status as requiring possession of interests or conscious awareness. The basic flaw is that there is no general agreement on what conscious awareness is. As Alisdair McIntyre might put it: Whose consciousness? Which awareness?

One notion implicit and sometimes explicit in the consciousness theory is that it requires some conscious person to be conscious of another person's consciousness: Practically speaking, only those who possess conscious awareness are qualified to bestow that state on some other being, like a monarch bestowing a knighthood by tapping the supplicant lightly on the shoulder with a sword. As recently as the mid-sixties, American blacks were deemed unfit to be received as fully qualified members of country clubs, fraternities, or professional organizations—they were deemed unfit by those who deemed themselves fit. But who deemed the "deemers" fit?

Ouspensky, in a monumental work on the subject, described seven layers of consciousness and indicated that most of us dwell all our lives on the third or fourth relatively primitive level; it is only by dint of enormous mental effort or a touch of the divine that we may ascend to the fifth level of consciousness. Visionaries, prophets, gurus, saints, and martyrs dwell on the sixth level; no one has ever approached the seventh level.

Mystic? Perhaps. But before we get too comfortable with the more concrete, commonly accepted physiology of conscious awareness, consider the matter of Karen Quinlan. She lay in a persistent vegetative state for nine years before expiring (she was helped along to eternity by her loving family), and in those years the most learned neurologists assumed that her cerebral cortex—the matrix in which our thinking or consciousness is said to reside—had been fatally damaged. Imagine their surprise when her autopsy report revealed that the major neurologic damage she had suffered was not to her cortex at all, which was relatively intact. Was she conscious? Was she thinking? How would we know?

There is immense and contentious literature on artificial intelligence, addressing the question of whether supercomputers have or may have the capacity for conscious awareness. Much of it is skeptical. Gelernter, in his eloquent, occasionally even lyric work, *The Must in the Machine,* remarks: "We ultimately might build a computer that seems to us to have a mind. But I doubt whether the computer itself will ever be taken in." But there is just as powerful a set of theories and experts arguing for computer consciousness. I could outline the debate at length, but what would it matter?

The essence of the computer qua mind debate is that it is contingent—as contingent as the disagreement concerning the existence of God. The pro-life community doesn't get bogged down in esoteric *pilpel* on what constitutes personhood and the question of whether conscious awareness is necessary for personhood. The pro-life community states very simply that we are all human beings and that no one quality can be depended upon to confer "personhood" upon us based on physical or mental attributes or skills. Needless to say, not everyone is so generous in the bestowal of the right to life. Philosopher Michael Tooley, for example, has constructed a list of fourteen attributes he believes necessary before the mantle of "personhood" should be bestowed. They are the capacity to experience pleasure/pain; the capacity for having desires; the capacity to remember past events; the capacity for having expectations with respect to future events; an awareness of the passage of time; the property of being a continuing conscious self... constructed in a minimal way, as nothing more than a construct of appropriately related mental states; the property of being a continuing conscious self, construed as a pure ego; the capacity for self-consciousness; the property of having mental states that involve propositional attitudes such as beliefs and desires; the capacity of having thought episodes; the capacity for reasoning; problem-solving ability; the capacity for using language; and the ability to interact with others.

Candidly, on a bad hair day, I am not at all certain I could meet such stiff requirements for personhood—if those are the minimal requirements, we're certainly talking about high admission standards. A vulnerable fetus—forget it! As Tooley himself summed up: "If the line of thought pursued above is correct, neither abortion, nor infanticide, at least during the first weeks after birth is morally wrong."

Another theory of the moral status of the fetus rests on via-bility—when it can exist outside the womb. Grobstein, in "Sci-ence and the Unborn: Choosing Human Futures," suggests that the fetal status blossoms into protectability and moral weight at the end of the twenty-sixth week of pregnancy, basing this on the observation that "this is close to the time of statistically reli-able viability with existing life-support technology." Again, a lamentably contingent proposal: Time has already passed him by. Viability at this writing is down to twenty-two weeks and moving south, and it is not unlikely that with further work on extra-corporeal membrane oxygenation and liquid breathing (the use of oxygen dissolved in perfluorocarbons, for the fetus to breathe in and extract oxygen much as a fish does with its gill structure—this work is going on at Temple University and seems to hold promise toward reducing the viability threshold into the late teen-weeks), viability will be down to the twenti-eth week by the trimillenium. Grobstein hedges his bets by throwing in other largely gratuitous observations: that at twenty-two weeks thalamo-cortical connections in the fetal brain have been established, but it is not until thirty weeks that the fetal brain shows "maturational changes" in its EEG, and he concludes with an old saw:

> The major impact would be that presumed inner awareness rather than viability would then be the key criterion for the definition of status.

We are back to Steinbok—though Grobstein pretends to a grander, loftier argumentation.

I HAVE CONTINUED TO WRESTLE with the question of the moral status of the fetus, and I have come to embrace an idea that is strikingly unlike either of those we have been discussing. To me, the most compelling factor establishing that the embryo, even at the earliest stages, before implantation in the uterus is an autonomous (though dependent) human agent of moral consequence is the "vector theory of life."

Here is how the *Webster's International Unabridged Dictionary* defines *vector:* "a complex entity representative of a directed magnitude, as of a force or velocity and represented by any of a system of equal and parallel segments." By vector of life, I mean the forces and velocities of life, directed to a specific end.

As early as 1971, Dr. M. Winnick recognized that the steepest slope of growth was in the first seventeen to nineteen days after fertilization: with respect to weight, protein content of the embryo. After nineteen days, growth of the organism slows because it is now dependent not so much on cell division (hyperplasia) but growth of the individual cells themselves (hypertrophy). The final phase of human growth is concerned with hypertrophy alone, *and this phase persists through adolescence into adulthood.* From that point on there is less hypertrophy (and no hyperplasia of any significance unless one is unfortunate enough to be incubating a tumor), and growth, to all intents and purposes, ceases. Indeed, in the geriatric phase of our lives, cells shrink and we are consequently severely physically diminished.

Add to this biological tumult the element of organization— that these rapidly dividing cells know exactly where to position themselves: armies of cells directed by a set of genes and enzyme systems contained within the chromosomal context of the preimplantation embryo very much akin to the Hox genes found in lower animals and positively identified as the directors of the assemblage. J. M. W. Slack has termed this the "fate map." Of this period, he stated, "it is not birth, marriage or death but gastrulation which is the most important time of your life." (To be fair: gastrulation, the splitting of the embryonic mass of cells into three well-defined layers of cells from which all structures, organs, appendages, and assorted other anatomical phenomena derive, does not actually commence until perhaps thirteen or fourteen days after conception. Preparations for the event, however, have been in progress since that momentous switch at the four- to eight-cell phase when control of genetic events passes from maternal influences to the embryo's exclusive control.)

Thus from the seeming chaos of early rapid-fire cell division and unimaginably precise deployment of these cells to their designated posts, there is a vector of life: a direction and velocity of life forces that is perfectly programmed, irresistibly logical, and immutably fixed in time and space. Critics of the vector of life theorem are fond of pointing out that it is not always thus: there are miscarriages generally attributable to errors in chromosomal division; there are congenital malformations ascribable to imprecision in the placement and posting of certain categories of cells, and there are even disappearances of embryos. (It is estimated that as many as one-quarter to one-half of twins will disappear as the pregnancy wears on.) But despite these infrequent biologic maloccurrences, the vast majority of embryos make it to birth as intact, perfectly formed human beings, having ridden the crest of the vector of life as a surfer rides the perfect wave. The vector is set in its most positive position in our earliest days, and insidiously swings to the directly negative pole as we age and finally confront death. That biologic vector is the sum of the forces and velocities of life at any given moment, and it is at its most glorious (and most mysterious) when we are morphologically very little, not even visible to the naked eye.

To SUM UP (PHILOSOPHERS CRINGE at this notion—there is no such thing as summing up; it is merely restating the argument): We have two general schemes upon which to posit moral status (read moral standing, respect, interests, claims, rights, weight, etc.). The subjective contingent criteria we have already discussed—i.e., conscious awareness, perception of pain/pleasure, the circular bestowal of moral status by those who already have it, and the exclusion from moral status of those the anointed believe should not have it. All of this is slippery, unquantifiable, and ultimately unreliable in its subjectivity, arbitrariness, and capriciousness. It is, in a word, terrifying.

On the other hand, we have a virtually unbroken series of quantifiable, noncontingent, scientifically verifiable and infinitely reproducible events that signifies the beginning of a new human life: the magnificently complex process of fertilization, the release of the factor PAF as the sperm penetrates the egg, the subtle change in the membrane structure of one or two of the early blastomeres to begin the "fate map," the momentous switch in control of embryonic events from maternal support to purely embryonic genetic substance, the overcoming of the "two-cell block" phase, the elaboration by the growing embryo of another chemical signal (human chorionic gonadotropin, or HCG) at the eight- to sixteen-cell stage (seven to eight days after fertilization), the equally dramatic process of implantation, and finally the omnipresent vector of life.

EMBRYOS ARE DEPENDENT CREATURES. So are fetuses. So are we all dependent: on the kindness or toleration of others, and on various biologic and medical devices (hearing aids, eyeglasses, dialysis, pacemakers—need I go on?). Surely, dependency is not a measure of moral standing; if it were, I venture to say that there would be perhaps two hundred or so people in the United States who qualify for full moral standing.

For myself, trained in the medical sciences and trusting more in the reproducible empirical data rather than some nebulous woolly subjective schema such as conscious awareness and personhood, I believe the fertilized ovum (zygote) to be a new individual launched along an unimaginably busy vector of life that terminates when the vector finally moves its 180 degrees to the negative pole. But I also concede that the design of the vector, the forces at play in the setting of the vector, and the subtle changes in the direction of the vector—these are matters beyond our understanding. It is not until we cede to the One who designed this magnificent master plan the credit we arrogate to ourselves for puzzling out each tiny piece in the plan—not until then—that any of us will achieve the full moral status we require to live together in peace and harmony—as He desires from us.

CHAPTER 11

The Silent Scream

WHEN ULTRASOUND IN THE EARLY 1970s confronted me with the sight of the embryo in a womb, I simply lost my faith in abortion on demand. I did not struggle to hold onto my old convictions. This change was, in its way, a clean and surgical conversion. I am by nature one who works out the conflicting data, weighs the opposing arguments with great care, makes a decision, and then acts upon it with no lingering backward glances.

By 1984, however, I had begun to ask myself more questions about abortion: What actually goes on in an abortion? I had done many, but abortion is a blind procedure. The doctor does not see what he is doing. He puts an instrument into a uterus and he turns on a motor, and a suction machines goes on and something is vacuumed out; it ends up as a little pile of meat in a gauze bag. I wanted to know what happened, so in 1984 I said to a friend of mine, who was doing fifteen or maybe twenty abortions a day, "Look, do me a favor, Jay. Next Saturday, when you are doing all these abortions, put an ultrasound device on the mother and tape it for me."

He did, and when he looked at the tapes with me in an editing studio, he was so affected that he never did another abortion. I, though I had not done an abortion in five years, was shaken to the very roots of my soul by what I saw. The tapes were amazing. Some of the tapes weren't of very good quality, but I selected one that was of better quality than the others and began to show it at pro-life gatherings around the country. (I had my first contact with the pro-life movement in 1981 when then president of the National Right to Life Committee, Carolyn Gerster, had gotten in touch with me.)

At the time, I was speaking at pro-life meetings around the country on weekends, and the response to the tape was so intense and dramatic that finally I was approached by a man named Don Smith, who wanted to make my tape into a film. I agreed that it would be a good idea. That is how *The Silent Scream,* which was to generate so much furor, came to be made. We showed it for the first time in Fort Lauderdale, Florida, on January 3, 1985. The reaction was instantaneous. Everybody was up in arms because *The Silent Scream* represented an enormous threat to the abortion forces and because it escalated the war (it's not really a debate—we don't debate each other; we scream at one another). For the first time, we had the technology and they had nothing.

The Silent Scream depicted a twelve-week-old fetus being torn to pieces in utero by the combination of suction and crushing instrumentation by the abortionist. It was so powerful that pro-choicers trotted out their heaviest hitters to denounce the tape. They very cleverly deflected the impact of the film into an academic cul de sac: a dispute regarding whether the fetus feels pain during an abortion. The impetus for the debate came from an on-the-record musing by then President Reagan as to how much pain the fetus feels during an abortion. (Actually, the video never mentioned the subject of fetal pain, and the transmogrification of the brutality depicted in the video into a rather jejune argument about the ability of the fetus to feel pain was a remarkably astute pro-choice strategy.)

Back and forth flew the arguments until the appearance of a state-of-the-art paper by K. J. S. Anand and coworkers at the Children's Hospital at Harvard Medical School. Anand stated:

> Cutaneous sensory receptors [for the perception of pain] appear in the perioral [around the mouth] area in the human fetus in the seventh week of gestation; they spread to the rest of the fetus, the palms of the hands and the soles of the feet by the eleventh week; to the trunk and the proximal parts of arms and legs by the fifteenth week and to all cutaneous and mucous surfaces by the twentieth week.

Anand goes on to state that synaptic connections between the pain receptor cells and the dorsal horn of the spinal cord appear at about six weeks of gestation but that the cells in the dorsal horn of the spinal cord do not begin to differentiate into their mature functional forms until thirteen weeks and are not fully matured until thirty weeks. In a similar vein, he states that the fetal neocortex begins to develop at eight weeks of gestation, and by twenty weeks each cortex (left and right) has its full complement of one billion neurons. In another section of this profound essay, Anand states that one of the more prominent neurotransmitter substances for the sensation of pain (he calls it P) appears in the dorsal ganglia of the cord and in the dorsal horns of the cord at twelve to sixteen weeks' gestation. He continues, "A high density of substance P fibers and cells has been observed in a multiple area of the fetal brain stem associated with the pathways for pain perception and control and the visceral reactions to pain."

Is Anand saying here that the fetus feels pain? Well, yes and no. Certainly the physiologic framework and the chemical substances for the perception of pain are present, but the maturing of these systems brings with it an increasingly sophisticated reaction to the perception of pain; if the fetus is exposed to a noxious stimulus (and one must bear in mind that the quantification of pain is still poorly understood, that human reaction to noxious stimuli is so variable, and that the endogenous opoid systems that enable us to control perceived pain only begin to develop at thirteen to fifteen weeks), it will undoubtedly perceive the pain. But how it understands it, whether it will remember it, whether it will act appropriately to mitigate it—these are all matters contingent on a mass of biological variables, some of which are still unidentified or poorly understood. In short, there are no satisfactory answers. Au fond, Anand's paper, illuminating and scholarly as it is, provides no answer for the argument of whether the human fetus feels pain—and it clearly does not speak to the question of what is a "person," who has "moral status," who has "interests," and when.

Is someone who feels little or no pain (a patient under anesthesia, a cancer victim having undergone dorsal rhizotomy, or a chronic invalid on heavy analgesic medication) somehow diminished in the personhood sweepstakes? My father disdained all forms of dental anesthesia, while I, like Oscar Wilde, must enter the dentist's office sagging on the arms of two nuns. Have I thus attained a higher level of personhood?

But the fetal pain cul de sac wasn't the only tactic of the pro-choicers when *The Silent Scream* appeared. They insisted that the video had been produced by manipulation. We were subjected to a number of editorials to this effect. Finally, we sent the tape to Dr. Ian Donald in Scotland, the man who had invented ultrasound, and who was a very old man at the time. I told Dr. Donald that we wanted his honest opinion: Had this tape been manipulated in any way, shape, or form? I told him that the *New York Times* had run several editorials saying that it was a fake. Donald looked at the tape and said that it was absolutely genuine. He swore an affidavit (which I still have) to that effect. I also asked Dr. Jay Kellinson, who had performed the abortion, if the film had been manipulated. "No," he replied, "it was all as you see it." Despite all the controversy, I believe that *The Silent Scream* was a powerful tool. It failed to change the minds of the lawmakers, but I think—and I say this humbly—that it has saved the lives of some babies. At least, I hope it has.

As I write this, I am a visiting scholar at the Center for Clinical and Research Ethics at Vanderbilt University, where I am pursuing a course of study that will lead to a master's degree in biomedical ethics. And I am still not satisfied with the disingenuous and unedifying answers to gnawing questions. I have often been asked, in the course of my innumerable lectures around the world: Doctor, if you knew there was a growing human being, a defenseless baby in the womb, and if you knew that you were either murdering it with your own hands or presiding over trained residents who were killing it with their hands, how, as a physician with even the rudiments of conscience and ethics, could you condone this work for all those years?

The answer is complex, enigmatic, and—I fear—self-serving.

Recall the times, if you will: The war in Vietnam was raging; and the countercultural, antiwar movement was so strong that it forced the nation out of that war and created a moral and political vacuum of antiauthoritarianism so potent as to threaten the very underpinnings of this republic. There was no countervailing moral factor in the balance. In reality, we knew very little about the fetus and had never seen it except as chopped-up, dismembered flesh or as a just-delivered infant. Consequently, the piteous flight of the unwillingly pregnant woman facing a dangerous, illegal abortion dominated our thinking.

One of the people with whom I discussed this is a philosopher who deals with matters known through the senses and immediate experience rather than through thought or intuition. I put the question directly to him: Were not all the explanations merely disguises for the mechanism of denial, the unwillingness to face the enormity of what we had done?

He replied that my question is at least in part a phenomenological one: We had tested the patient for pregnancy and had known that without question she was indeed pregnant, that there was a living human being within her, and we had destroyed that human being deliberately and without remorse. However, we had probably stumbled into the same phenomenological dilemma as had the early fifteenth century anatomists who preceded Vesalius. Vigegano, one of those early anatomists, who had published the first illustrated anatomical text after having dissected the human body, had persisted in drawing things he could not possibly have seen. He painstakingly described and illustrated a five-lobed liver, even though we know that the liver has only four lobes. Vigegano did this because he viewed the human body—open as it was to his objective and disinterested search—through the lens of Galen

(138–201 A.D.), the Greek physician whose antiquated anatomical and therapeutic theories and practices prevailed throughout the western world until the eighteenth century.

Fifteenth-century anatomists were still so mesmerized by galenic authority that they rejected the empirical evidence gathered through their own senses. They saw in the dissection of the human body what Galen (who had never actually dissected a human body) would have expected them to see. In somewhat the same way, perhaps the failure of those of us in the abortion movement to understand precisely what it was we were doing probably rests on what Kuhn has described as a "paradigm revision." This is the inability or resistance of the scientist to match discovery and theory: We saw the shards of tissue recovered from the procedure we had just finished, and yet we were unwilling or unable to abandon the old paradigm and claim the new—that we had in fact just destroyed a human life.

And so I am constrained to add that although we had a mound (literally) of empirical data attesting to the fact that a living human being had been destroyed in the act of abortion, it was not until after the advent of ultrasound technology that a true paradigm change took place. With ultrasound technology, we could not only know that the fetus was a functioning organism, but we could also measure its vital functions, effectively weigh it and estimate its age, watch it swallow and urinate, view it in its sleeping and waking states, and watch it move itself as purposefully as a newborn.

There is another way of knowing right from wrong. "Blessed are those who have not seen, yet believe." But we did not have that way. Without the shock value of overwhelming empirical evidence, and indeed the direct emotional impact that can be produced perhaps by no other sight than a human infant, none of us had the solid inner core of spiritual strength necessary to remind us of the enormity of the evil we were perpetrating.

It was at this point that I myself, confronted with this empirical revolution, this increasing mass of new data, began the painful process of changing my mind on the acceptability of abortion. I had finally accepted the paradigm shift.

In conversations with many of my original recruits, I have observed some hesitation, some reluctance to discuss the subject of abortion; many of these physicians who were once so eager to participate in the assembly line of destruction today voice a partially muted regret, a constellation of gathering doubts concerning the events of the early seventies at that clinic. It is not that they are publicly pro-life as I have now been for fifteen years, but the moral certainty is no longer there. A few no longer do abortions because of these doubts.

CHAPTER 12

To the Thanatoriums

DONALD STONER, THE RESIDENT who in 1957 killed himself and thereby provided me with my chief resident's job at Woman's Hospital, was a Californian who had come East with his wife several years earlier. He was an introspective, intelligent young man but became embroiled in an affair with one of the female residents in the program; it was also bruited about that he was simultaneously involved in a homosexual affair with another resident. Characteristically, Stoner gave no indication that he was unhappy or depressed. He killed himself in a manner eerily prophetic: He lay down on his couch, wrote out a brief note to the medical examiner of New York explaining what drugs he was using (he left no other notes), and then hooked up an intravenous infusion into his vein. The infusion contained sodium pentothal, a rapid-acting barbiturate used widely by anesthesiologists to put patients to sleep for surgery. He then hooked into the first infusion's rubber tubing a second infusion containing a massive dose of curare, a drug that paralyzes all the muscles of the body (including the diaphragm and respiratory muscles), and connected a timing device to the second infusion so that he would be fully asleep when the second fatal infusion began to run into his vein.

This method of suicide has been copied or modified by many of those who advocate the active killing of terminally ill patients. Dr. Jack Kevorkian first utilized a device very similar to Stoner's, but instead of using curare he used potassium chloride, an equally lethal drug as *his* agent of choice. Kevorkian is a retired morphologic pathologist, and morphologic pathologists deal for the most part with dead people.

At this writing Kevorkian is running amuck again, having helped to kill more than twenty people, usually described as "gravely ill." What counts as grave for the good doctor? Well, for instance, herpes, an inconsequential viral infection, generally sexually transmitted and of absolutely no medical significance unless it turns up in active form in a woman in labor in which case it *may* be transmitted to the newborn who *may* suffer devastating brain damage. Another of his suffering subjects was said to be in considerable pain from widespread arthritis. Rather than fumble about with temporary measures such as analgesic drugs (e.g., aspirin or Advil), the good doctor struck out boldly to get at the "root cause" of the problem (life) and eased her into the next world with such loving measures as carbon monoxide inhalation and other scientifically refined, highly technical modalities such as a plastic bag over the head.

MAIMONIDES'S LETTER TO AL-AFDAL, son of the caliph of Cairo, on the management of health, written in response to the nobleman's complaints of a variety of bodily and emotional ailments including constipation, indigestion, "bad thoughts," general anxiety, and a fear of death, adumbrated a lengthy list of dos and don'ts: He forbade truffles; warned against garlic, chick-peas, and unleavened bread; waggled the figurative finger at focaccio, water-fowl, young pigeons, and dates; and advised at least one bath a week. How much simpler and more confuting to have advised the young man to find a comfortable spot and pull a well-fitting plastic bag over his head.

It is all of an ineffaceably sad and sordid piece: We *think* we can create life in the laboratory (actually all we do is bring the component pieces into contact with each other and measure the miracle) and therefore we think we can *take* life on an equally rational and empirical basis. What dialectical ingenuity it requires to believe in such nonsense! Ironically, we are now beginning to understand that the end of life is a series of miracles as well: Accompanying the pain and the seeping away of energy in the terminal phases of illness is the outpouring into the bloodstream of a class of chemicals called endorphins, a variety of opiates (morphine-like substances) that calm us, alleviate the pain, and even allow us to exult in the knowledge that we have been loaned the gift of life and now the loan is being called. What we truly need is not more carbon monoxide and plastic bags, but a massive project dedicated to study the end of life as thoroughly and as scientifically as we have studied its beginnings. Only through such a study can we begin to apprehend the ineffable symmetry of the arc of life, something far beyond the ability of man's fumbling efforts to duplicate. Only a loving God could, I think, design a trajectory as perfect and as purposeful.

The Jack Kevorkians, the Planned Parenthoods, and the state of Oregon (and any other state so ethically disadvantaged as to condone physician-assisted suicide) will intersect at some grisly point on the ordinate of history. Drawing largely from my experience with a similar brand of pagan excess I predict that entrepreneurs will set up multiple small, discreet infirmaries for those who wish, have been talked into, coerced into, or medically deceived into death. The infirmaries (high-priced public relations experts will undoubtedly coin a term much more artful and euphemistic: perhaps "thanatorium," or even "infusorium") will be staffed with bright-eyed young men and women clad in crisp and crackling whites, solicitous and rhapsodizing as Waugh's Mr. Joyboy. These "counselors" will have the disadvantage of not having gone through the experience themselves (at my abortion clinic all "counselors" had to have had at least one abortion in order to qualify for the job) but will more than make up for that minor deficiency with their corporate compassion and impeccable manners. And there will be doctors and nurses there: the usual dirtbag of medical failures, misfits, alcoholics, drug addicts, and sexual perverts that I inherited when I took over my abortion clinic twenty-six years ago. (In short order I cleaned *them* out and substituted technically proficient, highly accredited practitioners suffering from vices no more objectionable than a unifying collegial venality, a secular humanism lethally stifling in its benignity, and a cupidity so colossal that it dwarfed any and all purely medical considerations, let alone philosophic ones.)

The "procedure rooms" in the thanatorium will be aseptic, but tarted up with the counterfeit articles designed to create a homey environment that one sees in the "birthing rooms" on obstetric units in hospitals across this nation: fake antique clocks on the wall, plaid bedcovers, and ersatz early American furniture so transparently bogus as to qualify as opéra bouffe. But that will be only in the first phase. As the thanatoria flourish and expand into chains and franchised operations, the accountants will eventually assume command, slashing expenses and overhead as competition grows. The final streamlined, efficient, and economically flawless version of the thanatorium will resemble nothing so much as the assembly-line factories that abortion clinics have become, and—farther on down the slope—the ovens of Auschwitz.

Nor will the phenomenon confine itself to the borders of the United States. Robert Latimer, a Canadian farmer from the province of Saskatchewan, in November 1994 performed an act of murder on his twelve-year-old daughter suffering from cerebral palsy; a Canadian court found him guilty of second-degree murder and he was sentenced to life in prison, with eligibility for parole in ten years. Predictably, Marilynne Seguin, executive director of Dying with Dignity (a group of activists advocating physician-assisted suicide) declared that the entire Latimer family had lived under a ghastly sentence for the entire twelve years of the daughter's life and she (Seguin) found the sentence of ten additional years of punishment unconscionable. When asked to comment on the matter, Eike Kluge, a professor of bioethics at the University of Victoria in British Columbia, ventured that active killing of such disabled youngsters could be decriminalized "under carefully controlled conditions." It is now a reasonable certainty that when the Canadian House of Commons meets this year, an item high on the agenda will be to strike down laws that presently outlaw the practice of physician-assisted suicide, or even active medical killing.

As a physician in practice for thirty-five years, I have yet to see anyone die with the trendy type of "dignity" that Seguin's group advocates. There is very little dignity to be discovered in the frantic thrashings of the poor benighted soul being smothered with a plastic bag over the head. Dying itself is a natural act, and immanent in the act is a perfect dignity that needs no help from us; God designed our lives, in His wisdom, to end in all manner of ways, and each way—irrespective of how untidy or disorganized it may seem to us—is inherently as dignified as any other.

Derek Humphrey's book, *Final Exit,* lists a dozen or so recipes for dignified dying by drug ingestion. I wonder if he has seen the fatally drugged patient in the last throes of life: the loud Cheyne-Stokes snoring that accompanies the attempt to maintain respiration; the spittle oozing from the corner of the mouth as the last moments approach; the convulsions induced in some victims as the terminal act of the death with "dignity"; the death rattle; the loosening of the sphincters with the passage of feces, gas, and urine; or the meticulous stuffing of the body orifices once the "dignified" death has supervened to ensure that no further body secretions escape to taint the air and tarnish the high moral tone of the act.

In 1986, in Florida where Patricia Rosier was suffering from metastic lung cancer, she and her husband, Peter—a respected and knowledgeable physician—planned for her a death with dignity: The family had a final meal together, she said her goodbyes to her two teenage children, and then she retired and quietly swallowed twenty Seconal (barbiturate) capsules. Her husband sat talking to her until she lost consciousness. But something went terribly wrong—she was unusually resistant to the barbiturate, and her husband had to facilitate her passage by giving a helping hand in the form of a double dose of morphine. By all accounts she was a fairly strong woman with a redoubtable will to live, and now the whole sad fiasco began to take on the trappings of a French bedroom farce: Into this pathetic scenario crept her stepfather, Vincent Delman, who, realizing belatedly that neither the Seconal nor the morphine had done the job, mercifully and presumably with great dignity, smothered her with a pillow (there appeared to be no fresh dry-cleaning in the house, and thus no plastic bag available).

Now here we have the ideal scenario for a deliberate, minutely planned death with dignity: a willing and dying woman, a devoted husband (a pathologist who should know more of the technical aspects of death-dealing than any of the other specialties in medicine), and a supportive family. Yet with all that technical know-how, volunteerism, and goodwill, the poor woman had to die like Desdemona, though not nearly as eloquently.

And always, the accountants lie in wait for us, armed to the teeth with their tendentious claims about cost savings to be anticipated if advance directives, hospice care, and the elimination of "futile (we shall return to consider the meaning of *that* word shortly) care" were actively practiced. In February 1994, Emanuel and Emanuel at Harvard Medical School published a comprehensive review of the world's literature on these matters and concluded as follows: "None of the individual cost-savings at the end of life associated with advance directive, hospice care or the elimination of futile care are definitive. Yet they all point in the same direction: cost savings due to changes in practice at the end of life are not likely to be substantial. The amount that might be saved by reducing the use of aggressive life-sustaining interventions for dying patients is at most 3.3 percent of total national health care expenditures." So much for the practical aspects of the economics of dying; the stark utilitarian approach to difficult bioethical problems that presently dominates the health care dialogue falls on its nose, at least in this one critical area.

To return to the medical "futility" issue for a moment, there are two generally understood meanings to the term:

(a) intervention without physical effect on the patient, which is referred to as "physiological futility," i.e., it will not have the effect sought by the intervenor, and

(b) interventions that have a demonstrable value, but which disinterested parties claim will have no benefit to the patient. This is often referred to in bioethical circles as "normative futility" but is actually a value judgment.

For example, unconscious life will be prolonged by the ventilator but the value of that life is open to debate. Which brings us to the chilling debate raging among the deep thinkers in this area regarding the "value of life."

In this plutonic climate, the intellectually anointed are engaged in trying to "operationalize" the quality of life. In short, there is a concerted movement among the bioethical bean counters to work out a calculus of what they term "quals," i.e., units quantifying the value of a given life. They have gone about this project (assigning qual units to any given life) by scoring the patient according to how the patient feels, how handicapped the patient finds himself as a result of the illness, how well he functions on an everyday basis, how much pain he is suffering, and how depressed/unhappy he may feel as a result of the illness. Each item is weighted with respect to its importance to the patient, and the aggregate is then pulled into a score.

The alternate means of calculating quals is to encourage the patients to express the utility they attach to the loss or gain of some specific function or ability—the so-called standard gamble approach. In this scoring system, one may be asked questions such as: How many years of your life are you willing to give up in order to live the remainder of your life in an ambulatory fashion? What risk of death would you accept? What would you give up to avoid this state? (Some illnesses and incapacities are theoretically worse than death.) The patient can then be scored according to the answers given.

Is that terrifying enough for you? The economists have also dipped *their* oars into this stygian sea. They have launched a project innocently titled "cost-utility analysis." This is a variation of a cost-benefit analysis; forget justice and autonomy, let's party with pure undiluted utilitarianism. Here, utility is measured by the benefits one derives from every dollar invested in health care, i.e., how many life-years (quals) we can save by investing in a new device. Economists now refer to this matter as "quality-adjusted years." For example, if the use of a new medication for the treatment of high blood pressure causes headaches, lethargy, or sexual dysfunction, this will tend to diminish the quality-adjusted years of life, so a new calculation of a functional year on this medication will be only 359 days instead of 365. Or, to put it in the stark mathematical terms the economists love so dearly, consider this expression:

$$\frac{\text{dollars}}{\text{quality of life years (adjusted)}}$$

As a concrete example, if the proposed new hypertension medication adds 6 years of life to the patient population but males become impotent and females get raging headaches from it, then one must adjust the calculated benefit downward (i.e., 4.3 or 3.9 years, depending upon how much weight the patient population awards to these undesirable side effects). Based on that calculation a decision will be made (always the passive voice at such moments, the syntax has been changed to protect the guilty) as to whether or not the new medication can or should be used. Please understand that thus far no major decisions have been made using this methodology in the United States, but the practice is common in Great Britain.

Do you shudder at the application of a jejune mathematical formula to determine the life and death of the sick person? Do you wonder where is individual choice, where is the doctor as patient advocate? Precisely. Welcome to the trimillenium.

CHAPTER 13

Nothing Wasted

IN 1987, FIFTEEN YEARS AFTER I had left the Center for Reproductive and Sexual Health (aka Women's Services, dba the largest abortion clinic in the western world), I received in the mail the following anonymous communication:

9/10/87
Dear Dr. Nathanson:

I am writing to you because I know you changed your mind on abortion since I worked for you in your clinic on 73rd street in the early seventies. I'm a Roman Catholic and I know I am sinning, but I still firmly believe that women have to have their reproductive rights. But what is going on now at the clinic I work at turns even *me* off. They do a lot of second trimester procedures here and I know you recently made a documentary [*Eclipse of Reason*] on that—but what you don't know is that they are now discussing with some business people about selling the tissue and the parts. I overheard them discussing this last week and they are even charging more for brain tissue than arms and legs and other parts.

As I said, I believe women should have control of their own bodies so abortion is legally and morally right although I know what the church says, but I believe the selling of these little parts is wrong. I can't tell you where I work or they'd fire me, and I need the job and really believe I'm serving women, but this is going TOO FAR.

P.S. You were always a good and fair boss and an honest man, so although I disagree with you now [on the abortion issue] I still respect you.

The letter was postmarked New York City and the word "Personal" was scrawled across the back flap of the envelope; someone somewhere had, in a groping, inchoate manner apprehended the first tentative slip down that (admittedly overworked) descending staircase to hell.

In the November 1992 issue of the generally well-regarded *New England Journal of Medicine,* there appeared a spate of scientific papers emanating from Yale University, McGill University, the University of Colorado Health Sciences Center, and the University Hospital of Lund, Sweden, claiming that human fetal nerve tissue had been used successfully to alleviate Parkinson's disease. In the treatment, the fetal tissue was transplanted into the brains of the Parkinson's victims. Predictably, this aroused simultaneously an enormous surge of hope from victims of this affliction and their families (there are at present one million victims of this disorder in the United States) and a heated debate on the moral acceptability of using human tissue as a means of treating disease in others. Not widely reported was that the study included only thirteen patients—a group so small that it invites the term "anecdotal." And yet the investigators concluded on the basis of this tiny aliquot of experimental subjects that further experimentation with the use of the fetal tissue was not only justifiable but morally mandatory. In the intervening three years there have been no reports in the general medical literature regarding the final outcome of the treatment of these patients, nor any reports of further work in this area.

The absence of any reports on follow-up studies on these and similar patients is regrettably reminiscent of the flurry of interest created by Madrazo et al., following reports of their work on tissue transplants into the brains of Parkinson's sufferers. Although there was an initial dramatic improvement in their condition, by the end of one year virtually all subjects had reverted to their "living statue" state. Many neurologists believe that these temporary improvements are caused not by any special property of the transplanted tissue but by the trauma and recovery from the operation itself. The wounds from the injecting needles temporarily stimulate the production of the neurotransmitter substance dopamine (the substance in short supply in Parkinson's disease) by the healing brain cells and tissue to create the temporary illusion of a "cure."

The landscape of medical history is littered with similar "miracle cures" and heartbreaking disappointments; in my own specialty (obstetrics and gynecology), the very serious disorder often termed "toxemia of pregnancy" has been known since Hippocrates's time. Glowing reports of success in treating this potentially fatal (to both mother and fetus) illness have included such "rational therapy" as mastectomy, oophorectomy (removal of the maternal ovaries), decapsulation of the maternal kidney, trephination (drilling a hole in the maternal skull), and aligning the woman with the earth's magnetic field with her head pointing toward the North Pole. The cure of tuberculosis by the "touching" of a monarch evolved into what Ryan, in *The Forgotten Plague,* describes as a "ceremony of vast proportions," and while Charles II of England was in exile in Holland his touch was in such demand that a number of consumptives were trampled to death in the rush to contact him. Interestingly, Samuel Johnson, a man of imposing intellectual credentials, was one of the last sufferers to be "touched" by Queen Anne.

The history of the use of fetal tissue transplants to cure adult disease is a long and remarkably ignoble one. Perhaps the most comprehensive recounting of that history can be found in the encyclopedic work of Peter McCullagh. In 1910, Shattuck reported on the experimental transplantation of fetal rabbit bones to humans (a dismal failure). In 1928, Fischera transplanted pancreatic tissue from three human fetuses into an eighteen-year-old male with diabetes, but the recipient died three days later in a diabetic coma. In 1935, Selle published a series of papers that described his attempt to reverse diabetes in depancreatized dogs by using transplanted fragments of human fetal pancreas, and Willis in the same year reported on his experiments with the transplantation of human fetal brain tissue into rats. After repeated failures, this line of experimentation was relegated to the medical waste bin for many years.

However, in the late 1970s, privately funded experimenters began reporting on the use of fetal tissue for the treatment of early-onset adult diabetes. Many of the experiments were funded by the Kroc Foundation, which derived *its* funding from the McDonald's hamburger chain. The results of these experiments were again uniformly disappointing, and in 1986 the Kroc Foundation was dissolved; a significant portion of the funds left in the foundation, upon dissolution, was distributed to researchers in the field of fetal tissue experimentation. When using the tissues of others to supplant the failing function of one's own, fetal tissue is most desirable since it provokes the least rejection reaction from the recipient. When foreign tissue is placed in one's body, the immune system attempts to destroy the foreign tissue. In the case of the placement of *fetal* tissue, the immune system reacts only weakly and the tissue may continue to function for weeks or months. In the case of the transplantation of fetal brain tissue into the sufferer of Parkinson's disease, the *Medical Letter on Drugs and Therapeutics* had this to say in 1993:

> No serious complications have been reported, and some studies suggested that the grafts were still functioning a year or more later (G.V. Sawle, et al., *Ann Neurology*, 1992, 31:166). Symptomatic improvement was uneven however—from one symptom to another, one patient to another, and one center to another—and often marginal; typically these patients still had *prominent signs of Parkinsonism, and none became asymptomatic* [italics added]. Many questions remain to be answered about the technique.

Nevertheless, advocates of fetal tissue experimentation continue to beat the drum not only for its potential for curing Parkinson's but in the treatment of a multiplicity of other neurologic disorders for which we have now no satisfactory treatment: strokes, paraplegia, Alzheimer's disease, multiple sclerosis, cerebral palsy, etc., as well as diabetes. As far back as 1985 Dr. Kevin J. Lafferty at the University of Colorado transplanted fetal pancreatic tissue into three adult diabetics with uniformly dismal results, and we have seen no significant improvement in the past ten years.

Moreover, it seems clear now that this technology demands tissues from a freshly aborted fetus. In the matter of diabetes, the fetus must be aborted between fourteen and twenty weeks in order for the pancreatic tissue harvested from the fetus to be suitable and functional. There are approximately 1.4 million insulin-dependent diabetics in this country, and it requires the tissue from eight fetuses to substitute for the deficient pancreas in the adult suffering from diabetes; thus we would need to abort 11.2 million fetuses annually at the fourteen- to twenty-week stage to treat all the insulin-dependent diabetics in the United States. At present we abort approximately 120,000 fetuses annually within this time window in pregnancy; where are the more than 11 million other fetuses to be sacrificed for this purpose to come from?

In the matter of the treatment of neurologic disease, as indicated earlier, there are approximately one million sufferers of Parkinson's disease in this country. In addition, there are at least one million sufferers of Alzheimer's disease, one million cerebral palsy patients, several million stroke victims and paraplegics, as well as 250,000 to 350,000 victims of multiple sclerosis. Thus we have at least four to five million potential patients awaiting fetal tissue therapy for their neurologic afflictions. Theoretically, in order to obtain suitable brain and nerve tissue for each patient, we must abort four fetuses at nine to twelve weeks, but 10 percent to 20 percent of the obtained tissue must be discarded because of bacterial contamination;

thus in practical terms we must abort *five* fetuses at nine to twelve weeks to treat each victim of neurologic disease with this technology. In short, we need to abort fifteen to twenty million babies at nine to twelve weeks to harvest sufficient tissue to treat this seemingly endless waiting list. We now abort approximately 800,000 babies annually in this time window of pregnancy; where are the other fourteen to nineteen million fetuses to come from? And with the advent of RU-486 (the abortion pill), probably 50 percent of women will choose medical abortion. These fetuses are already dead when expelled and are of no use for transplant purposes. Thus we must double all the figures cited once RU-486 comes into common use.

The answer, of course, is as simple as it is repugnant: We will be forced to buy and import unimaginable quantities of human fetal tissue from the third world. Entrepreneurs from the United States (and Western Europe as well) will flood Africa, the Indian subcontinent, and Central and South America, and will encourage women to become pregnant three and four times a year for the sole purpose of selling their fetal tissue. The sale of human tissue is prohibited in the United States, but such niceties are not observed in many underdeveloped countries. Even if the importation of such tissue into this country *were* barred, one can be sure economic and medical desperation alone would encourage a massive smuggling operation. Even now we cannot keep hundreds and thousands of tons of cocaine out of this country, not to mention hundreds of thousands of illegal immigrants. As long ago as April 1993 the Sansum Clinic announced that it planned to import fetal tissue from Russia. Unfortunately, the financial details of the proposed transaction were not revealed.

As to the economics and potential profits of this technology, consider that the placement of fetal brain tissue into the brain of a sufferer from Parkinson's disease is not simply a matter of sticking a needle into the skull of the patient and injecting the cells. First patients suitable for the technique must be screened (the doctors, nurses, and laboratory technicians necessary for this phase of the operation are all well paid). The abortions must then be performed (five for each patient awaiting the transplant), and of course the abortion doctors, and clinic and hospital personnel are compensated for their services. The tissue must then be immediately iced by a technician standing right at the abortion table (also paid), and then the tissue must be transported to a suitable laboratory where another technician will examine all the fetal tissue under microscope and winnow out the fetal neurons (nerve cells) appropriate for transplant (that technician is especially well paid since this is critical tedious work). The tissue is then processed and prepared for the actual transplant (another costly operation). Meanwhile the patient is also being prepared for the transplant by the doctors, nurses, nurse's aides, housekeeping personnel, social workers, and counselors to the patient and the family—all expensive items in the ledger. The actual transplant may then go forward under CT scan guidance (a special and very costly X-ray technique) by a neurosurgeon (they do not come cheap), specially trained operating room nurses and X-ray technicians (perhaps the most expensive phase of the technology), with an anesthesiologist involved (more dollars). The patient is then wheeled to a recovery area to be tended by nurses and doctors specially trained to recognize adverse effects of the procedure and to know how to deal with them (again, more dollars). Finally, the patient must be observed in the short and long term regarding the efficacy of the procedure, any adverse effects in the long term (personality changes, bleeding into the brain, infection in the brain, etc.), again with a substantial layout of funds. The patient may need a second transplant, if the first one misses the tiny designated area, and the register starts to ring again. What would *one* such procedure cost? Try $50,000 as a start, and then multiply that by five million (the number of potential subjects for fetal nerve tissue transplant) on the waiting list; that comes to $250 billion. We have not yet begun to discuss the economics of fetal pancreatic transplants for diabetics; bone marrow and liver transplants using fetal tissue; or fetus-to-fetus stem-cell transplants in utero for fetuses genetically destined to suffer from Hurler's syndrome (a connective tissue disorder), sickle-cell anemia, and a host of other genetically determined disorders that could be treated by stem-cell transplants from one fetus to another. Is this a reasonable allocation of limited resources—especially in light of the dubious efficacy of this technology?

Clearly not, yet just as clearly there is a large incentive for getting the procedure approved. With everyone involved in the process, from abortionist to social worker, profiting, it is preposterous to believe that a ban on "commercialization" of fetal tissue would

(a) remove the profit motive from this technology,

(b) reduce the demand for the technology, and

(c) at a stroke, sanitize the technology ethically—if the tissue cannot be bought or sold, then clearly it is an ethically acceptable procedure. (Is abortion any more ethically acceptable if the abortionist or the clinic waive the fee?)

If we require twelve million or so fetal cadavers at the fourteen- to twenty-week time window to treat all the insulin-dependent diabetics in this country with pancreatic fetal transplants, why waste the remainder of the fetus—after all, we have removed only one tiny organ for this procedure. Waste not, want not. Why not transplant fetal skin to the burned—or fetal hair to the bald? (We have no imperative to confine fetal transplant therapy *only* to the sick and disabled.) Why not give those with a flagging libido a transplant of fetal gonads? How about fetal teeth to the edentulous? Why not the routine transplant of a fresh, new fetal organ for a failing senescent adult one? Ultimately, we would be left, after the organ harvesting, with millions and millions of pounds of fetal carcass: muscle, cartilage, and connective tissue. Why not utilize this unimaginably rich source of protein and other nutrients to feed the homeless, to export to the third world (whence most of it came) to feed the suffering victims of famine—certainly this would not be cannibalism, since abortion rights proponents insist that the fetus is not a person or a living human being. Certainly it would be a more morally persuasive use of fetal tissue than, say, hair replacement would be; and on current evidence fetal tissue would be far more effective in preventing starvation than it is likely to be in curing disease.

The prospects of real, or at least unique and substantial, benefits from fetal research or tissue therapy are sufficiently far-fetched to make one wonder about the motives of its advocates. Yes, as noted, there is money to be made just as there is money being made on other expensive, high-tech, but dubiously effective medical procedures. But is this enough to explain the drumbeat for such an intrinsically horrifying endeavor? So horrifying indeed that one suspects the horror may be part of the motive; the horror or at least the thrill of shattering another taboo. Is there a will to the grotesque?

It is impossible to separate the issue of abortion from the use of the tissue obtained therefrom. If German physicians had harvested vital tissues and organs from the six million Jewish victims of the Holocaust and used them to save gravely wounded German soldiers, that good effect would in no way have mitigated the horror or excused the murders. Between August 1942 and May 1943 male prisoners at the Dachau concentration camp were lowered into an ice-water bath in order to gather data on hypothermia that would be potentially useful in the design of clothing and equipment for German soldiers in temperature extremes. The "research subjects" were held as long as seven hours in the freezing water, and one-third of the subjects died during the experiments. Dr. Josef Mengele, from 1943 to 1945, carried out experiments on twins, dwarfs, and prisoners with other assorted genetic anomalies, and a considerable corpus of data was amassed with these experiments. Leaving aside the issue of the scientific design of the experiments (grievously flawed, for the most part) and the validity and reliability of the conclusions flowing from those data (fragile at best, and largely unreliable at worst), the manner in which the experiments were conducted and the data collected were so irretrievably tainted that ordinary conscience forbids the use of these data. Indeed, in March 1988 Lee Thomas, the chief of the Environmental Protection Agency, barred from an EPA report on a particular toxic gas any data that the Nazis acquired in experiments on concentration camp subjects with toxic gases.

In every scientific paper dealing with the efficacy of fetal tissue transplantation, the abortionist is always listed as a co-author.

Moreover, there is no doubt that the medical use of fetal tissue would cause the number of abortions to increase. Even leaving aside the all-too-real possibility of third-world fetus farms, it has been my experience—based on seventy-five thousand abortions—that a great many pregnant women remain in doubt even to the door of the abortion clinic. (This accounts for the success sidewalk counselors have in diverting so many women from the abortion chambers.) If the abortion counselors could fire the cannon of altruism ("This abortion will not be in vain—we are going to see to it that the tissues of this fetus serve to save other lives"), surely the number of women who consent to the abortion would rise.

Humans are an end, *not* merely a means. That fetal tissue might be put to good use in research or even saving human lives does not trump this fundamental principle of Judeo-Christian law any more than the infamous Tuskegee experiment was justified by the unique data collected on the natural history of untreated syphilis, or the Willowbrook experiment was sanitized by the invaluable information harvested from the deliberate injection of live hepatitis virus into mentally retarded inmates.

The Son of Sam law in New York state forbids a class A felon from profiting from his criminal activity: A criminal's proceeds from the sale of a book about the crime, for instance, revert to the court and finally to the family of the victim. In short, the agent of the misdeed forfeits all rights to profits from that misdeed. Similarly, a mother may not sell her aborted fetus, but that will be no bar to other economic benefits disguised as part of the procedure (just as happens with "free-market" adoptions now). Moreover, the ban on the sale or marketing of this tissue does not a priori sanctify the technology; there are other self-interests at play here, e.g., the conception of a child merely for the purpose of aborting it and harvesting the vital organs for transplantation into another child of the same mother. This is not unprecedented. To cite only one example, there is the Ayala case in California in which a middle-aged couple with a child dying of leukemia conceived another child for the sole purpose of harvesting the bone marrow of the newborn for transplantation into the sick child. The project succeeded.

Fetal brain tissue is primitive and relatively undifferentiated. It is not unreasonable to propose that transplants of such tissue into adult brains may proliferate, creating a second mind within the original brain. This possibility is both admitted and defended by advocates of the procedure such as Mahowald:

> [B]etter to live with another's (partial) identity than not to live at all. Life is the more fundamental value, on which identify itself depends.

Then why not pursue more promising, less ethically disturbing avenues by which to promote this essentially utilitarian dogma? A new drug, Deprenyl, has been shown to have great promise in the treatment of Parkinson's. The drug was originally developed in Hungary in the sixties as an antidepressant: It works by nullifying the action of an enzyme in the brain that breaks down dopamine (in short supply in Parkinson's). Early testing has been, to say the least, propitious. Also, glial cell–derived neurotrophic factor (GDNF) has now been identified as a tonic to reverse the natural course of neurodegenerative diseases; this substance shows great promise in the treatment of Parkinson's disease. Dr. Latinen in Sweden has been destroying hyperactive neurons in a tiny area of the brain called the pallidum, and claims success rates in the range of 80 percent to 90 percent in the treatment of Parkinson's disease.

DR. ROGER GOSDEN, a researcher at Edinburgh University in Scotland, announced one year ago that he had taken ovaries from mouse fetuses, transplanted them into adult mice, and proved that the eggs in the fetal ovary could be fertilized and could develop into normal mice. He further indicated that he saw no significant barrier to performing the same biologic sleight-of-hand in humans, i.e., using fetal ovaries from aborted fetuses as a source of eggs for fertilization in the in vitro fertilization procedure (he predicted this technology would be feasible in humans in three years). In an editorial in *Fertility and Sterility,* Shushan and Schenker working in Tel Aviv enthusiastically endorsed this biologic grotesquerie. But even the ultraliberal wing of the U.S. bioethical community reacted with outrage and dismay. George Annas, an ethicist and lawyer at Boston University who is customarily open to the most fecklessly hogarthian schemes, figuratively screamed, "The idea is so grotesque as to be unbelievable," and "It is one thing to want to have a child, but there are limits."

Where are they? Where do they come from?

CHAPTER 14

Abortion and Violence

I HAVE JUST FINISHED READING a volume on the abortion conflict that is perhaps the most thoughtful, balanced, and judicious account of the struggle written to this date; I refer to the book *Before the Shooting Begins* by James Davison Hunter, who is a professor of sociology at the University of Virginia, and who deals with the cultural war surrounding the abortion issue.

Regrettably, however, the shooting has already begun. The list of victims (I exclude the thirty million tiny human beings who have been exterminated in the abortion chambers) commences with the fatal shooting of Dr. Michael Gunn by Michael Griffin in Pensacola, Florida, in March 1993; it continues with the nonfatal shooting of Dr. George Tiller in Wichita, Kansas, in August 1993 (he was wounded in both arms) by Rachelle Shannon, an anti-abortion activist who resides in Grant's Pass, Oregon; and it moves forward inexorably to the murders of Dr. John Britton, the abortionist at another Pensacola clinic, and James H. Barrett, a retired Air Force colonel who was serving as a volunteer escort for women entering the Pensacola Ladies Center in Pensacola for the purpose of abortion, by Paul Hill, a former Protestant minister and anti-abortion activist. Hill also wounded Barrett's wife June, sixty-eight, with the twelve-gauge shotgun he wielded. The casualty list lengthens with the shooting of Dr. Garson Romalis, a gynecologist working at an abortion clinic in Vancouver, British Columbia. Dr. Romalis was shot, not at his abortion clinic but through the window of his home in suburban Vancouver; it remains unclear as to whether this was the work of an anti-abortion activist, although two leading anti-abortion groups in British Columbia have roundly denounced the shooting. Finally, John Salvi III, an emotionally volatile, seemingly confused twenty-two-year-old prospective hairdresser shot and killed two workers at two abortion clinics in Brookline, Massachusetts, and wounded five others, then turned up the next day in Norfolk, Virginia, where he proceeded to enfilade the Hillcrest abortion clinic in that city. Fortunately, no one was injured or killed in the Virginia campaign.

In addition there have been more than one hundred documented instances of arson, firebombings, and other potentially deadly assaults upon the facilities themselves over the past twenty years.

Is this the entirety of the list? Will the killings stop, now that Michael Griffin is serving a life term in prison, Paul Hill was convicted of two counts of murder and was sentenced to execution in Florida, Rachelle Shannon was convicted of attempted first-degree murder following her assault on Dr. Tiller and is now serving an eleven-year prison term in Kansas, and John Salvi had been indicted in Massachusetts on two counts of murder and five counts of attempted murder?

Regrettably, the answer is no, the killings will probably not stop.

On May 15, 1993, I received a copy of a letter addressed to President Clinton, written by one Dennis Drew in Chicago and postmarked May 14, 1993. It opens as follows:

> Dear President Clinton:
>
> I will kill you if that is the only way to stop you from <u>personally</u> [underlining in original] and imminently killing a viable fetus in New York state which has no feticide law, if that fetus could be born alive without significant health risk to the mother.

The letter rambles pathetically on, largely incoherently, for three pages; there is one other section, however, that is arresting:

> If the federal government declines to prosecute my threat, and <u>still</u> no one makes a legal move to stop the killing of viable babies that could easily be born alive, I may have to do a Michael Griffin [the killer of Dr. Gunn]. I won't kill anybody. I won't even use a weapon. I may "put a rocket in somebody's pocket." I may have to break some New York state abortionist's arm. Sorry.

I did not report this threat-missive to the authorities, in that according to Mr. Drew copies of it had been sent to the *New York Post,* the "ACLJ" (probably the ACLU), and "200 other luminaries." Nevertheless it was an occasion for some significant brow-furrowing.

When I received a copy of the October 1994 issue of *The Progressive* magazine, I recognized again the venomous lunatic passions that the abortion struggle qua cultural war is capable of arousing. There was an article headed "Anti-Abortionists and White Supremacists Make Common Cause," by Loretta J. Ross, national program research director for the Atlanta-based Center for Democratic Renewal, which styles itself as "a clearinghouse for information on hate groups and bigoted violence." The magazine is flagrantly pro-abortion, and the article equates Randall Terry, formerly director of Operation Rescue, with such lunatic fringe figures as Paul Hill, Michael Griffin, and leaders of such extremist groups as the KKK, Aryan Nation, and American Front (a Portland-based group of neo-nazi skinheads). That comparison is itself a little demented: I know Randall Terry quite well, well enough to respect his motives, to know that he is a spiritual, deeply dedicated person, committed body and soul to nonviolence.

But what struck me in the article was the following passage:

> The White Patriot Party, formerly the confederate knights of the KKK, issued a death threat against Dr. Bernard Nathanson in June 1985 in a newspaper called the Confederate Leader: "Jew abortion king Bernard Nathanson of New York City, was tried, convicted and sentenced to death by hanging, by a fair and unbiased [*sic*] judge and jury of the White Patriots on May 19 in Siler City, North Carolina. Nathanson was convicted of 55,000 counts of first-degree murder, treason against the United States of America and conspiracy to commit genocide against the White Race."

Evidently the White Patriot Party has been limited in its communications to smoke signals (I had by that time been on the pro-life side of the abortion conflict for at least five years) or else they must be the most petulantly unforgiving bunch since Thomas de Torquemada and his deranged successor, Diego Deza. In any case, I am informed by the authorities that, despite my modest contributions to the pro-life cause, the death sentence is still dismayingly prominent in the alleged minds of the White Patriots.

NOT SINCE THE SLAVERY ISSUE and the rise of the abolitionist movement has there been a comparably combustible cultural war in this nation. In the run up to the Civil War, there was also a decades-long string of increasingly frequent and violent incidents. And although the pro-slavery side got its licks in early and often, from the mob murder of abolitionist journalist-minister Elijah P. Lovejoy in 1837 to the near fatal caning of Charles Sumner by Preston Brooks on the floor of the Senate in 1856 as the prewar conflict evolved, it was the fanatics among the abolitionists who often initiated the violence, from Unitarian minister Thomas Wentworth Higginson's two attempts in 1851 and 1854 to forcibly release fugitive slaves from federal custody to John Brown's deadly raid on a pro-slavery village on the Pottawatomie Creek in Kansas and his suicidal attack on the federal arsenal at Harpers Ferry, Virginia, in 1859, which culminated in the deaths of two of Brown's sons and his own hanging six months later.

These most well-known incidents are but a fraction of the multiple incidents of violence during the slavery conflict. Many of the incidents were attributable to well-intentioned fanatics like Brown, who were out of touch with reason and rational discussion; others were the works of persons with no stock in the slavery issue but who were seemingly carried along into violence by the *zeitgeist*.

Although there are many superficial dissimilarities between the questions of abortion and slavery, there is one core issue at the epicenter of these struggles common to both: the definition in moral terms of a human being and the sweep of natural rights that accompanies that status.

In the case of slavery, that issue was sharpened to a razor's edge and brought unbearably on point by the U.S. Supreme Court's 1857 *Dred Scott* decision, which declared blacks, in effect, nonhuman, property. Free or slave, said Roger B. Taney, the chief justice of the Court who wrote the majority opinion, blacks could not be citizens of the United States and therefore could have no legal standing before the Court. Further, he wrote, "Negroes are so inferior that they had no rights which a white man was bound to respect," and then went on to liken the slave, as pure property, to a mule or a horse.

Taney, attempting to remove the issue from political debate, radically constricted the possibilities of compromise or discussion, virtually dictated the Lincoln–Douglas debates, and may have made the war inevitable.

Are we marching down that same bloodied road in the abortion conflict? There are disheartening signs that we are, and largely because of a very concrete failing in our politics that parallels *Dred Scott* and its aftermath.

Like *Dred Scott*, *Roe v. Wade*, which despite minor prevarications has been repeatedly reaffirmed by the Court, attempted to remove the abortion decision from politics and thus effectively radicalized the debate, discouraging compromise, political half-measures, or even edifying discussion. In particular it denied to pro-life forces the ordinary tools of politics. The declaration that abortion was for all practical purposes an inalienable constitutional right left pro-lifers unable to work the political trenches at the state level, or to push for statutory restrictions at the congressional level. They were left with only two options, one largely illusory.

Politically, they could pursue a constitutional amendment banning abortion. But as more pragmatic pro-lifers have repeatedly pointed out, the Human Life Amendment, as it is known, is an exercise in quixotic futility. In the absence of a national moral consensus on the issue, it is simply too large a step to be the first step. An America capable of passing a pro-life amendment would not need one; an America that needs one cannot possibly pass it.

So much for ordinary politics. The other alternative that seemed open to pro-lifers was to wage a war of conscience, to educate, advocate, and nonviolently protest the horror until the nation was moved to reconsider. Meanwhile, if the protesters, advocates, educators, and pamphleteers could not immediately move the nation at least they might save individual mothers and children from the monster. After all, reducing the number of abortions is a goal that all sides in the debate at least pretend to share. Even then-Governor Clinton, running for president, pledged to make abortion "safe, legal, and *rare.*"

In recent years, however, the avenue of peaceful protest, advocacy, and education has been more and more constricted as well.

We have a James Buchanan-like president in the White House who acknowledges that the horror should be at least reduced, but who is so politically indebted to the pro-choice side that since that one word, "rare," spoken in a debate, he has not in any way acknowledged any responsibility to address the issue.

Congress has been loathe even to debate the matter, though it was finally forced to a refreshing modicum of frankness during the debate over partial birth abortions. As for the media, at the risk of appearing self-serving, neither *The Silent Scream* nor *Eclipse of Reason,* my second documentary (on late-term abortions), have ever been shown on network TV. The networks have also refused to allow pro-life groups to buy time to air even the most innocuous pro-life ads, i.e., ads that do not even mention abortion but simply celebrate the choice of life.

Most disastrous, however, has been the legal and extralegal campaign to shut down pro-life protests, or even pro-life speech. The Freedom of Access to Clinic Entrances Act was designed not, as some claim, to thwart violence but in effect to silence peaceful protest and dampen or eliminate "sidewalk counseling," the (often successful) attempt to inform pregnant women on their way into abortion clinics of the truth of what they are about to do and to extend them any help necessary should they decide to keep their babies.

This is an insane policy, bound to increase violence against clinics, not reduce it. It has not been the peaceful protesters, the legitimate opposition, that has been responsible for the clinic violence: Michael Griffin and Paul Hill were lunatic fringe zealots who did no serious sidewalk counseling; had not thought the issues through carefully; and acted in a solitary, impulsive, and violent manner. It is as if the entire abolitionist movement were tarred with the extremist brush of John Brown, rather than being identified with the reasonable opposition voices of such luminaries as Wendell Phillips, John Greenleaf Whittier, and Rev. Theodore Parker. Or as if all civil rights protesters were made out to be Black Panthers, or if the anti-Vietnam War protesters were identified exclusively with the extremists who blew up the University of Wisconsin laboratory, killing a researcher. Increasingly, fanatics, activists with short fuses, and telescopically visioned zealots seeing no legitimate avenues of protest open to them will inevitably turn to violence as a last resort, encouraged by authority figures like the notorious priest David Trosch, who stated publicly that killing abortion doctors is "justifiable homicide." For a zealot precariously balanced on the very edge of sanity, wildly irresponsible remarks such as this are sufficient to precipitate a plunge into the dark, bloody grounds of social and political dementia.

Think of it this way: The cultural war is a vessel filled with water and put on a high flame. Normally there are outlets of political action and peaceful protest from which the steam may escape, but someone has blocked the escape valves while neglecting to turn off the flame. The vessel will inevitably explode like a grenade, spewing shards of metal and glass all over the vicinity—and someone will be hurt. This is precisely what led up to the climactic events of the Civil War—and we appear to be on that identical path now.

Hunter has made some eminently reasonable suggestions in the interests of containing the conflict, including the idea that if we downscale the political units at which the decision is made (i.e., from the federal government to the states), the debate might become more focused, specific, and less intractable. Democracy flourishes in a small-scale setting.

HUNTER'S APPROACH STANDS IN STARK CONTRAST to that of poseurs such as Lawrence Tribe and Roger Rosenblatt, who have each written widely publicized books claiming to represent the path of moderation on the issue. Each pretends to approach the subject of abortion with an entirely open mind (I wish I had a nickel for every time Tribe's name has appeared on an amicus brief favoring *Roe v. Wade*) and a disarming "who, me?" smile; each is pathetically transparent in his pro-abortion bias. The more disturbing problem with deep thinkers like Tribe and Rosenblatt, however, is that neither has been in the abortion arena, doing the abortions or, alternatively, demonstrating against them. The gravest error they make is the naive assumption that everyone is as purely secular and as sweetly reasonable as they. They fail to understand the depth of commitment to the cause, most especially on the pro-life side (which both regard with a thinly veiled contempt). Pro-life convictions spring from and have their roots in traditional Judeo-Christian values, in the Bible, and in the commanding concept of the immortal soul. For them to underestimate the virtually irresistible force of the provenance of that pro-life conviction is a fatal mistake—as fatal as believing that because the U.S. Supreme Court has declared it legal, abortion is moral. Like the nineteenth-century abolitionists, pro-life adherents hold the U.S. Supreme Court decision in great disdain.

In my criss-crossing of the United States over the past fifteen years speaking on the subject of abortion and allied issues, I would be met by one or more members of the local pro-life organization that had invited me to the city in question. Sometimes it would even be a small delegation of members—but in Midwest airports I would invariably see, on the fringes of the welcoming committees, a middle-aged man of unmemorable stature wearing a beige sailor-type hat adorned with pro-life slogans in the form of buttons, stickers, and inked messages.

I ignored him the first time or two I saw him—except to say a perfunctory hello accompanied by an equally perfunctory handshake—but I noticed that he turned up at virtually every major pro-life convention at which I was the designated main speaker.

When I met him the third or fourth time, I drew him aside and inquired of him why he wore that curious hat, with all the literature on it. He grinned at me, then explained that he was "Prolife Andy," an Air Force retiree.

I asked him what his *real* name was, and he replied that "Pro-life Andy" *was* his real name; he had had it changed legally from Charles Anderson. Then he proceeded to unbutton his shirt, roll up his sleeves, and elevate his pants legs: I saw a mass of pro-life slogans tattooed over virtually every inch of his visible skin! He identified himself as a walking testament to the pro-life cause, had dedicated his entire life to the cause after he'd left the Air Force several years earlier, and regretted only that he could not do more for the cause.

Andy is an unusual but not isolated example of the seemingly limitless passion and conviction this issue generates. I have encountered in my travels countless men and women who have relinquished promising careers in the professions, industry, education, social work, and theology to work full time on the abortion issue. Are they all crazy? Are they all ravening slavering zealots who will not be satisfied until they gun down an abortion provider or firebomb a clinic? No, no, and again no. These are supporters of a cause that is so close to the bone of their religious beliefs, of their moral and ethical centers, that the issue consumes them—but consistently in a nonviolent manner.

Resistance to injustice may take many forms. Henry David Thoreau wrote the following in his monumental treatise "Civil Disobedience":

Unjust laws exist. Shall we be content to obey them, or shall we endeavor to amend them and obey them until we have succeeded, or shall we transgress them at once? Men generally under such a government as this think that they ought to wait until they have persuaded the majority to alter them. They think that if they should resist the remedy would be worse than the evil. But it is the fault of the government itself that the remedy is worse than the evil. It makes it worse. Why is it not more apt to anticipate and provide for reform? Why does it not cherish its wise minority? Why does it cry and resist before it is hurt?... Why does it always crucify Christ, and excommunicate Copernicus and Luther, and pronounce Washington and Franklin rebels?

It is said that during his brief stay in a local jail (because he refused to pay a poll tax to support the war in Mexico in 1847) Thoreau was visited by Emerson, who was horrified at the sight of his old friend Thoreau behind bars and asked: "Henry, what are you doing in there?" Thoreau is said to have pointed his index finger at Emerson and to have replied: "Ralph, what are *you* doing out *there?*" Perhaps Emerson took the point. Speaking on slavery and the unjust Fugitive Slave Law to a New England audience, Emerson on January 25, 1855, stated the following:

Now what is the effect of this evil government?
To discredit government. When the public fails in its duty, private men take its place.... When the American government and courts are false to their trust, men disobey the government, put it in the wrong;

the government is forced into all manner of false and ridiculous attitudes. Men hear reason and truth from private men who have brave hearts and great minds. This is the compensation of bad government—the field it affords for illustrious men, and we have a great debt to the brave and faithful men who in the very hour and place of the evil act, made their protest for themselves and their countrymen, by word and by deed. They are justified and the law is condemned.

Emerson was speaking specifically of the slavery controversy (this was a scant six years before the outbreak of the Civil War), but the majestic sweep of his rhetoric encompasses every phylum, every genus, every species of man's inhumanity to man. It is strong rhetorical medicine; it applies in every sense to the principles at stake in the abortion conflict.

The pro-choice cadres seem to have no sense of the danger of the game they are playing in using federal power to suppress dissent. Recently they have trumpeted a demand for federal marshals to protect abortion clinics on the grounds that abortion is a constitutionally protected right and as such must be directly protected by federal agents. Leaving aside for the moment the fact that there are three thousand known operating abortion clinics in the United States (requiring at a minimum nine thousand marshals to post a single guard around the clock) or that a significant number of marshals would have serious conscientious objection to such duty, if we accept that the federal government is directly responsible for supplying security guards for the exercise of constitutional rights, then logically under the First Amendment every house of worship, every newspaper, and every peaceful assemblage of citizens would have a similar claim.

Predictably, in order to justify their extravagant demands for federal force, the pro-choicers have wheeled out that wobbly old vehicle, the conspiracy theory. (Oliver Stone, where are you now that we need you?) On a recent broadcast of the program *Nightline,* a discussion was held between Ted Koppel and Attorney General Janet Reno regarding the problem of abortion clinic violence. Koppel queried her as to whether Reno believed there was a conspiracy afoot to systematically kill off all the abortion providers in the United States. How this loony idea lodged itself in Koppel's otherwise well-organized and logical head is impossible to say. Reno responded with appropriate circumspection to the query—neither affirming nor denying it, but adroitly changing the subject in midsentence (she has evidently learned a valuable lesson or two in realpolitik since Waco). To imagine anyone attempting to draw into a conspiracy four such conspicuously unstable, disturbed loners as Shannon, Hill, Griffin, and Salvi is a paranoid notion so goofy as to deserve nothing but a tolerant smile and a nervous look over one's shoulder.

Still, even granting that serious thinkers will discard the conspiracy theory out of hand, the idea is in the air and will probably not lack for advocates, egged on by the pro-choice lobbying machine. Will pro-life conventions and assemblages then be viewed as covens of co-conspirators? Will every pro-life gathering be monitored, taped, and bugged by the FBI, the CIA, and by those overworked federal marshals? There is endless mischief in this notion.

The wisest move President Clinton could make on the domestic front would be to invite pro-life leaders into the White House for a daylong exchange of views. At a stroke this would calm the roiling waters of the abortion conflict; it would provide a badly needed escape valve for the massive head of pressure building in the frustrated oppressed pro-life legions and establish him as a receptive, broad-minded peacemaker on the domestic front.

True, he would get some flack from the pro-choice side, but the net result would, I believe, translate into significant political capital for him, especially in light of the returns from the 1994 midterm elections: recall, please, not a single pro-life incumbent member of Congress (or governor) of either party was defeated by a pro-choice challenger, but more than two dozen hard-core incumbent pro-choice members of Congress were defeated by pro-life challengers, and on net there was a shift of forty seats in the House and six seats in the Senate in the pro-life direction. Because the issue has been effectively removed from the political sphere by the Court, that electoral shift will not automatically have the effect it might be expected to in a democracy. But it stands for a political and moral passion too strong to be safely excluded from consideration by the nation's leaders if in fact they want to lead us to some resolution rather than simply wait for the firestorm.

CHAPTER 15

The Hand of God

I HAVE BEEN HOLDING LENGTHY conversations with a priest of
Opus Dei, Father John McCloskey, for the past five years, and
it is my hope that I shall soon be received into the Roman
Catholic Church. It was not supposed to work this way; the
whole unimaginable sequence has moved in reverse, like water
flowing uphill. The usual and customary progression is: Belief
in God and His splendid gift of life leads the believer to defend
it—and to become pro-life. With me, it was just the opposite:
Perversely, I journeyed from being pro-life to belief in God. I
was not seeking anything spiritual; my desires have been—for
the most part—earthly and of the flesh, my goals concrete and
tangible—and readily liquefiable into cash. To make matters
worse, I was openly contemptuous of all this as a stiff-backed
Jewish atheist, or as Richard Gilman would have taxonomized,
"a perfunctory Jew."

Getting from there to here wasn't easy. I went through a ten-
year "transitional time"—perhaps 1978–1988—when I felt the

burden of sin growing heavier and more insistent. It was as if the contents of the baggage of my life were mysteriously absorbed in some metaphysical moisture, making them bulkier, heavier, more weighty, and more impossible to bear. I found myself longing for a magical phlogiston, a substance that would contribute a negative weight to my heavy burden.

During this decade, it was the hour of the wolf that was the most trying time. I would awaken each morning at four or five o'clock, staring into the darkness and hoping (but not praying, yet) for a message to flare forth acquitting me before some invisible jury. After a suitable period of thwarted anticipation, I would once again turn on my bedside lamp, pick up the literature of sin (by this time I had accumulated a substantial store of it), and reread passages from St. Augustine's confessions (a staple), Dostoevski, Paul Tillich, Kierkegaard, Niebuhr, and even Lewis Mumford and Waldo Frank. St. Augustine spoke most starkly of my existential torment but, with no St. Monica to show me the way, I was seized by an unremitting black despair.

Suicide runs in my family. (Is there a gene for suicide?) My paternal grandfather and sister killed themselves, and my father made at least one attempt at suicide in his mid-forties. He had used tranquilizers and sleeping pills. My reading in those unbearably painful hours in the morning turned to what Camus once described as the central question of the twentieth century: whether or not to commit suicide. As a physician, I had the ability to write the necessary prescriptions to end my life. Was I up to the task?

Which was, of course, precisely the question posed by Prince Hamlet: Was it rank cowardice to commit suicide, or was it even more cowardly to shrink from the deed? And, like the good prince, I waffled into the decision of indecision: not yet. I reasoned that there were pragmatic considerations. I had patients who needed me (every physician comforts himself with the fantasy that he is irreplaceable to the patients), and there was pro-life work to be done. I knew there were cleaner hands to do this work, but I told myself that somewhere, someday, someone might profit from the story of the travails through which I was feeling my way.

Like the diagnostician I was trained to be, I commenced to analyze the patient's humors, the patient being myself. I determined that I was suffering from an affliction of the spirit; the disorder had arisen, at least in part, from an excess of existential freedom, and this had created a penumbral despair. I had been cast adrift in a limitless sea of sensual freedom—no sextant, no compass, no charts, simply the dimly apprehended stars of the prevailing penal code, an imitative grasp of the manners and mores of society (a chimpanzee could be trained to do as well), a minimalist concept of justice, and a stultified sense of decency. I required not a cure but healing.

I had performed many thousands of abortions on innocent children, and I had failed those whom I loved. Of my second and third marriages, I cannot write in any detail—it is still so painful for me. Suffice it to say that both of my spouses, though neither were churchgoers when we met, had retained a core of innocence from their Protestant childhoods that kept them pristine and curiously innocent—at least until I got my hands on them. At least my father, who died in 1990 at the epic age of ninety-four, had been reconciled before his death. My son Joseph was living in his grandfather's apartment and taking care of him at the time. My father had not believed in God but only in some "superior power." All his life he had proclaimed that he wanted nothing to do with primitive rituals like funerals. Thus it came as a surprise that his will stipulated that he was to be buried at the side of his daughter, whom he had in life reduced to less than a nonentity. I was making the arrangements for the cremation and was stunned when my niece produced a document verifying that he had bought the burial plot alongside my sister and had always planned to be buried there—despite his own proclamations to the contrary.

At the time of this writing, I have already tried the traditional panoply of secular remedies: alcohol, tranquilizers, self-help books, counseling. I had even indulged myself in four years of psychoanalysis in the early 1960s. The analyst was a highly respected psychiatrist who adhered largely to a Freudian model, contributing little while allowing the patient to babble on. Unfortunately, he suffered from a terrible case of hay fever year-round and took heavy doses of antihistamines. The result was that twice weekly I would slump on his couch excitedly recounting my dreams, while he would slump in his wide leather chair, snoozing peacefully from the antihistamines. After several sessions devoted to keeping him awake by surreptitiously kicking him, I, too, took to napping. (I was, in a perverse sense, sleeping with my psychiatrist.) I don't know why I clutched at this straw so long.

The keenest of human tortures is to be judged without a law, and mine had been a lawless universe. Santayana once wrote that the only true dignity of man is in his capacity to despise himself. I despised myself. Perhaps I had at least arrived at the beginning of the quest for human dignity. I had begun a serious self-examination (the examined life is barely worth living) and had begun to face the twisted moral homoculus reflected in the mirror of self-examination.

I knew now that the primary illness is the severing of the

links between sin and fault, between ethically corrupt action and the cost. There had been no concrete cost to my corrupt actions, only behavioral exegesis, and that would not do. I needed to be disciplined and educated. I had become as Hannah Arendt had described Eichmann: a collection of functions rather than an accountable human being.

At the same time, I was moving deeper into the pro-life movement with my lectures, films, books, and political activities. I perceived the sense of peace that emanated from so many of these people. But my pro-life views were scientifically based, and I made this clear to all audiences, even the most rigidly Catholic. At the prayers and invocations at pro-life rallies, I would unbend enough to recite the Pledge of Allegiance when it was called for, but the prayers found me with my eyes fixed rigidly in front of me, lips unmoving. Though pleasant and civil to the various clerics at these rallies, I made certain they knew that I held myself at a distance from their beliefs—except in our shared detestation of abortion. Nevertheless, there was an indefinable air of selflessness, even genuine altruism, at the gatherings that I noted with marked interest.

Then I attended an action by Operation Rescue against Planned Parenthood in New York City in 1989. I was planning an article to be published in an ethics journal on the moral and ethical aspects of such demonstrations: Were they legitimate protests or domestic terrorism—that is, the denial of constitutionally based rights to pregnant women?

The morning of the Rescue was bitterly cold. I joined the legion, approximately twelve hundred demonstrators, at their rendezvous in the west forties in Manhattan and proceeded with them by subway and foot to the clinic on Second Avenue and Twenty-first Street. They sat themselves down in rows in front of the clinic, effectively blocking entrances to and exits from the abortion clinic. They began to sing hymns softly, joining hands and swaying from the waist. I circulated on the periphery at first, observing the faces, interviewing some of the participants, making notes furiously. It was only then that I apprehended the exaltation, the pure love on the faces of that shivering mass of people, surrounded as they were by hundreds of New York City policemen.

They prayed, they supported and encouraged each other, they sang hymns of joy, and they constantly reminded each other of the absolute prohibition against violence. It was, I suppose, the sheer intensity of the love and prayer that astonished me: They prayed for the unborn babies, for the confused and frightened pregnant women, and for the doctors and nurses in the clinic. They even prayed for the police and the media who were covering the event. They prayed for each other but never for themselves. And I wondered: How can these people give of themselves for a constituency that is (and always will be) mute, invisible, and unable to thank them?

After I wrote my article and it was published in the Hastings Center Report, several pro-choicers accused me of having taken an active part in the demonstration, in violation of an injunction against such activity issued by federal Judge Robert Ward. I was tried and cleared in a federal court in New York. At the same time, my wife was charged with violating another injunction against demonstrating at an abortion clinic in Dobbs Ferry. We settled her case, and between the two cases, it was expensive, though I certainly don't regret a nickel of it. I observed a subsequent demonstration in New Orleans and another in a small town south of Los Angeles. I was shaken by the intensity of the spirituality at these demonstrations. The demonstrations were ecumenical, with as many Catholics as Protestants, and nonviolent, and they were so deeply rooted in spiritual conviction that even the police hung back, in deference, I believe, to the purity of the action. The only brutality I personally witnessed at the California rally was committed by female police officers, who seemed personally offended by the demonstrators. (Randall Terry, the founder of Operation Rescue, later assured me that indeed female officers are especially aggressive at these demonstrations; they hated the demonstrators individually and collectively.)

Now, I had not been immune to the religious fervor of the pro-life movement. I had been aware in the early and mid-eighties that a great many of the Catholics and Protestants in the ranks had prayed for me, were praying for me, and I was not unmoved as time wore on. But it was not until I saw the spirit put to the test on those bitterly cold demonstration mornings, with pro-choicers hurling the most fulsome epithets at them, the police surrounding them, the media openly unsympathetic to their cause, the federal judiciary fining and jailing them, and municipal officials threatening them—all through it they sat smiling, quietly praying, singing, confident and righteous of their cause and ineradicably persuaded of their ultimate triumph—that I began seriously to question what indescribable Force generated them to this activity. Why, too, was I there? What had led me to this time and place? Was it the same Force that allowed them to sit serene and unafraid at the epicenter of legal, physical, ethical, and moral chaos?

And for the first time in my entire adult life, I began to entertain seriously the notion of God—a god who problematically had led me through the proverbial circles of hell, only to show me the way to redemption and mercy through His grace. The thought violated every eighteenth-century certainty I had cherished; it instantly converted my past into a vile bog of sin and evil; it indicted me and convicted me of high crimes against those who had loved me, and against those whom I did not even know; and simultaneously—miraculously—it held out a shimmering sliver of Hope to me, in the growing belief that Someone had died for my sins and my evil two millennia ago.

I did not instantly experience a blinding epiphany and begin to recite "Hail Marys" in the manner Richard Gilman described in *Faith, Sex, Mystery,* his sad, shabby little tale of conversion from Jewish atheism to Roman Catholicism, and who invoked all manner of magical and mystic coincidence. In my case, I was led to a searching review of the literature of conversion, including Karl Stern's *Pillar of Fire.* I also read Malcolm Muggeridge, Walker Percy, Graham Greene, C. S. Lewis, Cardinal Newman, and others. It was entirely in character with me that I would conduct a diligent review of literature before embarking on a mission as daunting and as threatening as this—searching for God. It was also a search for authenticity in what was—for me—a revolutionary enterprise.

I read voraciously. The two experiences with which I could most closely identify were Gilman's (we had almost identical backgrounds) and that of my former professor, Karl Stern. Although I reread Gilman several times, I found it irrelevant to my concerns: Gilman had converted to Catholicism at the age of thirty and then had been embarrassed by the conversion, even regarding it as an illness from which he had to recuperate. Gilman spoke frequently of the "pain" of being a Catholic. He also demonstrated a contempt and disdain for his surrender to such doctrines as that of the Trinity and the Incarnation. I found him immensely unhelpful. As for the undeniably brilliant Simone Weil, she thoroughly detested her Judaism, while I merely found mine unhelpful and inadequate.

Stern's experiences resonated much more forcefully with me. A brilliant psychoanalyst, he divests himself of all the paraphernalia of his intellectual and professional accomplishments and opens himself to a simple, unquestioning faith, as innocent as that of his heroine St. Teresa of Avila. Here was a man I would emulate—if I could. Following his conversion, Stern wrote a letter to his brother, who was then living in Israel, that is a paean to the discovery of Christian faith. Stern's letter to his brother is so eloquent and so sensitive to the doubts and questions of a trained professional such as himself. With each reading, I found myself fighting back the tears.

But, as Newman said, no one was ever converted by argument. At every pro-life rally at which I speak, I still apprehend the ecstatic faces, radiating such love and joy that I find an icy knot deep within me (Where? The pineal gland? The marrow of my bones? Does it matter?) slowly thawing into rhapsodic waves of warmth.

Like Simone Weil, I have found myself forever on the threshold of blessed surrender to faith but always reluctant to take the last, irrevocable step. Father McCloskey supports me and encourages me by paraphrasing the words Pascal uttered four hundred years ago: "The cost of believing in God is minimal; the consequences of doubt may be significant."

I am sure that Pascal did not mean this statement to represent some calculus of belief, and I repeat this to myself frequently during my waking hours, a conscious mantra. For I have such heavy moral baggage to drag into the next world that failing to believe would condemn me to an eternity perhaps more terrifying than anything Dante envisioned in his celebration of the redemptive fall and rise of Easter. I am afraid.

Although my fears are great, I know something now that I did not know. A few years ago, I was asked to review a book by an internist, Dr. Larry Dossey, who claimed to have adduced scientific proof that intercessory prayer works. I remained unconvinced by his data, but nevertheless one of the stories, that of Dossey's visit to a patient dying of cancer, has stuck with me. The man was constantly praying. When Dossey asked what he was praying for, the man said he wasn't praying for anything.

"Well," said Dossey, "if prayer isn't asking, then what is it for?"

"It isn't for anything," the patient replied. "It mainly reminds me that we are not alone."

I am no longer alone. It has been my fate to wander the globe in search of the One without Whom I am doomed, but now I seize the hem of His robe in desperation, in terror, in celestial access to the purest need I have ever known. My thoughts return to the hero of my medical school years, Karl Stern, who was undergoing a spiritual metamorphosis at the very time he was instructing me in the arts of the mind, its orders, and its sources, and the words he wrote in a letter to his brother:

"And there was no doubt about it," Stern wrote, "toward Him we had been running, or from Him we had been running away, but all the time He had been in the center of things."

Afterword

YOU HAVE JUST READ one of the more important autobiographies of the twentieth century. Through its several English editions and its Spanish edition *The Hand of God* has been made available to countless millions of readers in the Americas and in Spain. Other translations have been made or are in progress, including French, German, Polish, and Finnish. *The Hand of God* ranks with Thomas Merton's *Seven Storey Mountain* and Malcolm Muggeridge's *Chronicles of Wasted Time* as a book that our descendants, both familial and spiritual, will turn to in order to understand both man's inhumanity and the possibility of redemption. Merton, Muggeridge, and Nathanson, brilliant intellects all, came from atheistic backgrounds and succumbed to many of the ideological and carnal temptations of their age only to finish, through God's grace, as converts to the Catholic Church. I am sure that they would agree with Hilaire Belloc's words: "One thing in the world is different from all others. It has a personality and a force. It is recognized and (when recognized) most violently loved or hated. It is the Catholic Church. Within that household the human spirit has roof and hearth. Outside it, it is the night." And it was a dark and frigid night in the twentieth century.

The power and grace of this book is to be understood in the context of the teaching of the Catholic Church, which has stood—and stands—virtually alone in defense of the sacredness of human life from natural conception to natural death. In his encyclical *Evangelium Vitae* the Holy Fr. John Paul II has upheld the principle of the "dignity of the human person" in the face of a century of mass slaughter and degradation. The Holy Father is well aware of this book and knows its author personally. Dr. Nathanson's conversion to the cause of life and to Christianity is indeed highly significant as a witness to the power of scientific evidence, prayer, and the inexorable connection between God and the natural law that He has inscribed in the human mind and heart. As is happening increasingly in the United States and elsewhere, if you acknowledge and follow the natural law, you may very well find God and the Church.

During the late 1970s Dr. Nathanson became a favorite target of the anti-life cultural forces in America, the subject of ridicule and satire in comic strips and news commentary, and the butt of jokes of television comedians for his change of heart and mind regarding the objective reality of abortion, which he came to regard as the taking of innocent human lives, comparable to the Dachau of Hitler, the Gulag of Stalin, or the Cambodia of Pol Pot. Since then, along with maintaining a distinguished obstetric medical practice and university teaching, he has given hundreds of lectures throughout the world in defense of the unborn. Now in his seventies, he recently received a degree in medical bioethics, continuing his professional preparation and better arming himself to defend the cause of human life.

At the end of the book, however, our friend Dr. Nathanson has left us hanging. Did he indeed finally run toward Him from whom He had been running away even though all the time He had been at the center of things, to paraphrase his mentor and fellow convert, Dr. Karl Stern? The answer is yes. He reached the final goal—the beginning of eternal life in this life—which is found in the sacrament of Baptism.

On December 8, 1996, on a Monday at 7:30 A.M. on the solemnity of the Immaculate Conception in the crypt chapel of the Cathedral of St. Patrick's in New York City, the City of Man, Dr. Bernard Nathanson became a son of God, incorporated into the Mystical Body of Christ in his One Church. John Cardinal O'Connor administered to him the sacraments of Baptism, Confirmation, and Holy Communion. His godparents were Joan Andrews, a heroine of the pro-life movement who spent years in prison giving witness to the evils of abortion, and John Downing, an attorney, a close Catholic friend of some twenty-six years. His sponsor for confirmation was Chris Slattery, a man who had left a lucrative career in advertising to dedicate himself wholeheartedly to the cause of life by his direction of the only pro-life alternative for expectant women in Manhattan, the Crisis Pregnancy Center. In his homily, Cardinal O'Connor remarked that the lack of respect for life is rooted in a lack of self-respect, and that a lack of self-respect is a consequence of sin. How fitting it was, the Cardinal continued, that Dr. Nathanson should enter the Church on the feast of the new Eve.

Among the concelebrants were some of his friends, all well-known spokesmen for life both nationally and internationally: Fr. Paul Marx, the founder of Human Life International; Monsignor William Smith, perhaps the Church's leading moral theologian in the United States; and Fr. Richard Neuhaus, a former Lutheran minister who had been received into the Church by Cardinal O'Connor in 1989, and who is now the editor of one of the most influential religious journals in the United

States, *First Things*. Standing out among the various persons—most of them close friends—that Dr. Nathanson had invited was a stranger, a man Dr. Nathanson had never met, Chuck Colson. He traveled a long way to be there, in many senses. He is very well known in the United States as a major figure in the Watergate scandal of the 1970s, for which he spent several years in prison. There he had a conversion to evangelical Christianity and began a pastoral work with incarcerated men. Today he is perhaps the best known Evangelical Protestant leader in the United States, with a radio show and many books to his credit. He is also a principal author and signer of the "Evangelicals and Catholics Together" statement, which is an attempt on the part of Catholic and Evangelical leaders to high-light what unites them in Christ while at the same time attempting to move toward unity in what still separates them. Listen to Colson's impressions of that moment:

> This week I saw fresh and powerful evidence that the Savior born 2,000 years ago in a stable continues to trans-form the world. Last Monday I was invited to witness a baptism in a chapel of St. Patrick's cathedral in New York City. The candidate for baptism was none other than Bernard Nathanson, at one time one of the abortion industry's greatest leaders, a man who personally presided over some 75,000 abortions, including the abortion of his own child.... I watched as Nathanson walked to the altar. What a moment. Just like the first century—a Jewish con-vert coming forward in the catacombs to meet Christ. And his sponsor was Joan Andrews. Ironies abound. Joan is one of the pro-life movement's most outspoken warriors, a woman who spent five years in prison for her pro-life

activities. It was a sight that burned into my consciousness, because just above Cardinal O'Connor was a cross.... I looked at the cross and realized again that what the Gospel teaches is true: in Christ is the victory. He has overcome the world, and the gates of hell cannot prevail against his church.... And this is the way the abortion war will be won, through Jesus Christ changing hearts, one by one. No amount of political force, no government, no laws, no army of Planned Parenthood workers can ever stop that. It is the one thing that is absolutely invincible. That simple baptism, held without fanfare in the basement of a great cathedral, is a reminder that a holy Baby, born in a stable twenty centuries ago, defies the wisdom of man. He cannot be defeated.

But what was the reaction of Dr. Nathanson himself as he received the Sacraments of initiation into his new life as a Christian? "It was a very difficult moment. I was in a real whirlpool of emotion. And then there was this healing, cooling water on me, and soft voices, and an inexpressible sense of peace. I had found a safe place.... For so many years I was agitated, nervous, intense. My emotional metabolism was way up. Now I've achieved a sense of peace." At the end of the Mass, Cardinal O'Connor, in a comment that brought gentle laughter to the congregation, said to him, "There, now you're as Catholic as I am!" After the ceremony Dr. Nathanson's reaction, understandably, was one of gratitude: "I can't tell you how grateful I am, what an unrequitable debt I have, to those who prayed for me all those years when I was publicly announcing my atheism and lack of faith. They stubbornly, lovingly, prayed for me. I am convinced beyond any doubt that those prayers were heard. It brought tears to my eyes."

On the prayer card handed out at the Mass of his reception, Dr. Nathanson had one quote from Sacred Scripture, "God, who is rich in mercy" (Ephesians 2:4), the very same phrase that the Holy Father used as the title for his encyclical on God the Father, *Dives in Misericordia*. It certainly reflects his attitude as he faces his new life as a Catholic: "I'm confident about the future, whatever it may hold, because I've turned my life over to Christ. I don't have control anymore, and I don't want control. I made a mess of it; nobody could do worse than I did. I'm just in God's hands."

Several years after his Baptism, Dr. Nathanson retired from his flourishing medical practice in order to dedicate himself more fully to the cause of life. He has intensified his pro-life work throughout the world by means of writings, lectures, and expert witness testimony in court and in legislatures both here and abroad. But he has not restricted himself to fighting the continuing tragedy of legal abortion.

For Dr. Nathanson is not just an activist; he is a prophet.

As long ago as 1988—before he was a theist, much less a Catholic—Dr. Nathanson gave the keynote speech at an important Symposium on the Twentieth Anniversary of the Encyclical Humanae Vitae held at Princeton University. To a rapt and somewhat astonished audience, he spoke of what was soon to come as a result of the misuse of science and lack of respect for the sacredness of human life: genetic manipulation, sex selection, surrogate motherhood, frozen embryos, cloning, stem cell research, and the sale and use of body parts. All of his predictions have been borne out as the struggle between the Cultures of Life and Death continues. No one at that Princeton conference would have imagined that only ten years later the university's prize chair of Ethics would be held by Dr. Peter

Singer, an advocate of all of the above and much worse. We can be sure that Dr. Nathanson will continue to use his professional expertise and his newfound faith to defend the sacredness of human life, as Pope John Paul II puts it, "from conception until natural death."

Rev. C. J. McCloskey III
Washington, D.C.
December 12, 2000
Feast of Our Lady of Guadalupe
Patroness of the Unborn

Bibliography

E. Bykov, "Aspiration of the Gravid Uterus," *Vrach Delo* 9 (1927) 21.

N. F. Cantor, *The Sacred Chain: The History of the Jews* (New York City: Harper Collins, 1995).

G. Devereux, *A Study of Abortion in Primitive Societies* (London: Thomas Yoseloff, Ltd., 1960).

L. Dinnerstein, *Anti-Semitism in America* (Oxford University Press, 1994), 118.

E. J. Emanuel, "The Economics of Dying: The Illusion of Cost Savings at the End of Life," *New England Journal of Medicine* 330 (1994):540–544.

Freed et al., "Survival of Implanted Fetal Dopamine Cells and Neurologic Improvement 12 to 46 Months After Transplantation for Parkinson's Disease," *New England Journal of Medicine* 327 (November 1992):1549–1555.

D. Gelernter, *The Must in the Machine: Computerizing the Poetry of Human Thought* (New York: Free Press, 1994).

R. Gilman, *Faith, Sex, Mystery: A Memoir* (New York: Simon and Schuster, 1986).

D. Gimes, "Clinicians Who Provide Abortions: The Thinning Ranks," *Obstetrics and Gynecology* 80 (1992):719–723.

I. Gougeon and J. Myerson, *Emerson's Antislavery Writings* (Yale University Press, 1995), 102.

James D. Hunter, *Before the Shooting Begins* (Oxford, Sydney, New York: Free Press, 1994).

H. H. Knaus, "The Action of Pituitary Extract Upon the Pregnant Uterus of the Rabbit," *J Physiol* 6 (1926):383.

I. Madrazo, R. Franco-Bourland, F. Ostrofsky-Solis, et al., "Fetal Homotransplants (Ventral Mesencephalon and Adrenal Tissue) to the Striatum of Parkinsonian Subjects," *Arch Neurol* 47 (1990):1281–1285.

M. Mahowald, *Fetal Tissue Transplantation: An Update, in Bioethics and the Fetus* (New Jersey: Humana Press, 1991), 103–121.

Peter McCullagh, *The Fetus as Transplant Donor: Scientific, Social and Ethical Perspectives* (New York City: John Wiley and Sons, 1987).

The Medical Letter on Drugs and Therapeutics 35 (1993):103–104.

M. Moissides, "Contribution a L'etude de L'avortment dans L'antiquite Grecque," *Janus*, 26 (1922):59, 129.

B. Nathanson, "Suction Curettage for Early Abortion: Experience with 645 Cases," *Clinical Obstetrics and Gynecology* 14 (1971):99-106.

J. Noonan, *A Private Choice, Abortion in America in the Seventies* (New York: Free Press, 1979), 122.

J. G. Raymond, R. Klein, and L. J. Dumble, *RU-486, Misconceptions, Myths, and Morals* (IWT Press, 1991).

R. Rosenblatt, *Life Itself* (New York: Random House, 1992).

F. Ryan, *The Forgotten Plague: How the Battle Against Tuberculosis Was Won — And Lost* (Boston: Little Brown, Inc., 1993), 7–8.

A. Shushan and J. Schenker, "The Use of Oocyte Obtained from Aborted Fetuses in Egg Donation Programs," *Fertility and Sterility* 62 (1994):449–451.

D. D. Spencer et al., "Unilateral Transplantation of Human Fetal

Mesencephalic Tissue into the Caudate Nucleus of Patients with Parkinson's Disease," *New England Journal of Medicine* 327 (November 1992):1541–1546.

F. J. Taussig, *Abortion, Spontaneous and Induced* (C. V. Mosby Co., 1936).

Lawrence Tribe, *Abortion: The Clash of Absolutes* (New York: W. W. Norton and Company, 1990).

Robert M. Veatch, *Theory of Medical Ethics* (New York City: Basic Books, Inc., 1981):22–24.

H. Widner et al., "Bilateral Fetal Mesencephalic Grafting in Two Patients with Parkinsonism Induced by 1-Methyl-4-Phenyl-1,2,3,6-Tetrahydropyridine (MPTP)," *New England Journal of Medicine* 327 (November 1992):1556–1563.

Index